Beavers Bend Resort Park Area Guide

(Where to Stay, Where to Eat & What to Do)
"Oklahoma's Best Kept Secret"

By

Dave White

The photograph on the cover is of the
River Bend Area of the Beavers Bend Resort Park.
It was taken in early fall by the author. Note the
Cypress trees that are native only to this area of the state.

Beavers Bend Resort Park Area Guide

(Where to Stay, Where to Eat & What to Do)
"Oklahoma's Best Kept Secret"

Copyright 2005

Another **OUTBACK ADVENTURES BOOK**

Billy Dennis
OUTBACK ADVENTURE PRESS
7410 S. 58th W. Ave.
Tulsa, Oklahoma 74131

First Edition, 2005

Copyright © Pending

All rights reserved.
No part of this book may be reproduced
in any form or by any electronic or mechanical means,
including information storage and retrieval systems, without
the expressed permission in writing from the author and publisher.

ISBN 0-9768248-0-9

Manufactured in the USA by Thomson-Shore, Inc.
Dexter, Michigan

Contents

Preface 1
Acknowledgements 2
How To Use This Book 3
Emergency or Important Telephone Numbers 4
Average Temperature and Rainfall 5
Where is Beavers Bend Resort Located? 7
Park History 12
Area Pictures 15
Places To Stay (In the Park) 18
Places To Stay (Outside the Park) 22
Things To Do (Inside the Park) 36
Fishing Information 52
Things To Do (Outside the Park) 55
Gift Shops 74
Places To Eat 76
Services You Might Need 78
Where To Purchase Hunting/Fishing Licenses
And Land Use Permits 80
Church Services 80
Animals Native To Southeastern Oklahoma 83
About Outback Guides 91

Preface

Beavers Bend Resort Park is one of the top tourist destinations in the State of Oklahoma. Oklahoma Living Magazine, November 2004 issue, ranks it as the number one "Best Vacation Spot in Oklahoma". More than 450,000 people visit the park yearly taking advantage of the many varied activities offered within the Park and out side the Park. Water activities, hiking, golf, site seeing or just relaxing the Park offers a variety of choices that will appeal to both young and old. The more adventuresome can try out the Parks mountain biking trails or kayak the Mountain Fork River for a short distance of four miles, or an overnight trip of eighteen miles.

You will not find a better place in Oklahoma to trout fish. In fact many anglers come from Texas and Arkansas to try their luck. Whether you own an ATV or a horse you'll have hundreds of miles of state and privately owned land made available for public use through an agreement with the Oklahoma Department of Wildlife Conservation with numerous dirt roads, and logging roads to explore.

The purpose of this book is to help you take full advantage of all the area resources available for your fun and enjoyment. I've included such things as the best places to go ATVing or horseback riding, if this is your first time in the area where to try your luck at catching that big trout, best places to camp on the David Boren Hiking Trail (DBHT), and helpful information on which length kayak and canoe trip is right for you.

Park cabins are usually reserved one year in advance and campsites are on a first-come basis, so I've included a detailed list of cabins and campgrounds that are in close proximity to the park including amenities offered by each. Some are located near rivers for easy fishing; others are located right next to the ATV and horse trails.

For those wanting to try some of the local food there is a detailed map showing all the area restaurants location from the park and the type of cuisine that each specialize in.

So, if you need information on where to stay, what to do, or where to eat all you will need is this guide book.

Acknowledgements

I enjoyed working on this book—the first of many I hope to write about the Parks and hiking trails of Oklahoma. This book could not have been written without the help of a number of people. Foremost is Billy Dennis who realized a need for this book and encouraged me to write it.

Also of great help in the writing of this book were the Staff of Beavers Bend Resort, Terry Walker, Jim Miller and Michele Finch-Walker for giving suggestions for improvement and expressing their encouragement and support for this endeavor. Thanks also to Kyle Johnson, Honobia Creek/Three Rivers WMA biologist for reading over and pointing out changes to the section dealing with the Wildlife Management Areas and to B.J. at Hochatown Junction Resorts for her support and help. She made many suggestions on what to include in the book and helped put me in contact with many of the Broken Bow/Beavers Bend area people. Thanks also to Gena Jordan of Beavers Bend White Water Canoe and Kayak Rental whose helpful, cheerful and positive attitude helped immensely in the writing of this book. I received great help from K'Lynn and Dewayne Hall of Trail Hankie, LLC. Many of the maps in this book were drawn by them. They also advised me on how to start drawing my own maps for future books.

Most importantly I thank my wife Marilyn, who supported me and stood by me through the months it took to take this project from just an idea to a finished project.

> Outback Publishing is donating a portion of the proceeds of each book sold to, The Friends of Beaver Bend for the building of a new nature center and to the Oklahoma Department of Wildlife (Fisheries Dept.) to help preserve Oklahoma's land and wildlife for future generations to enjoy.

How To Use This Book

Within a thirty-five mile area surrounding Beavers Bend Resort Park there are a wide number of choices of where to stay, things to do and places to eat. This book is designed to help visitors to the area quickly find the information to make their stay enjoyable for all members of their family.

This guide is divided by activity. Wondering which cabin's are just right for you? Locate where each of the cabins are located on the map then read the cabin description. Whether you're looking for a small efficiency cabin or a large luxury cabin, the information is here to help you make that choice. Need even more information? Check out the cabins web site, look at the exterior and interior pictures of the cabins and if you need more information, we've provided the cabin operator's telephone number, just give them a call.

Activities are also divided into two areas; those within the Park and those outside the park. Maps showing their location from the Park are provide along with descriptions and telephone numbers you can call for even more information.

Also, provided are maps showing where restaurants, gift shops, museums and convenience stores are located in relation to the Park so you don't waste a lot of time driving around.

Finally, information on where to buy fishing and hunting licenses and land use permits as well as age and residence requirements are provided to make your stay as enjoyable and trouble-free as possible.

We hope the following pages will help you enjoy your vacation experience here in the Broken Bow and Beavers Bend Resort Park Area.

Emergency or Important Telephone Numbers

Emergency Only 911
OKLAHOMA POISON CONTROL 1 (800) 522-4611
Park Ranger .... (580) 494-6300
Major Emergency (EMS and Ambulance) .... (580) 584-2800
Minor Emergency (Nurse at Regional Hospital) .... (580) 286-7623
Fire (Hochatown) .... (580) 494-6333
Fire (Broken Bow) .... (580) 584-2424
Police (Broken Bow) .... (580) 584-9312
Lake/Highway Patrol .... (405) 924-2601
Sheriff (McCurtain County) Non-Emergency .... (580) 286-3331
U.S. Army Corps of Engineers .... (580) 494-6374

Beavers Bend Resort Park

Reservation Office .... (580) 494-6538
Forest Heritage Center .... (580) 494-6497
Lakeview Lodge .... (580) 494-6179
Beavers Bend Marina .... (580) 494-6455
Nature Center .... (580) 494-6556
Cedar Creek Golf Course .... (580) 494-6456
Administration Office .... (580) 494-6450
 .... (580) 494-6452
Beavers Bend Restaurant .... (580) 494-6551

Oklahoma Dept of Agriculture (Forestry Services) ..... (580) 584-3351
Wildlife Refuge .... (580) 584-6211
Tourism and Recreation Information 1 (800) 652-6552

Monthly Average Temperature and Rainfall for Broken Bow, OK

	Ave. High Temp. F	Ave. Low Temp. F	Ave. Precip.	Record Highs	Record Lows
Jan.	51.7°	26.9°	2.9"	78° (01/28/1975)	1° (01/31/1966)
Feb.	56.4°	31°	3.5"	89° (02/22/1996)	0° (02/04/1996)
Mar.	65.4°	39°	5.3"	89° (03/24/1995)	8° (03/10/1996)
Apr.	74.6°	48.4°	4.7"	95° (04/19/1987)	24° (04/03/1987)
May	74.6°	56.9°	6.6"	95° (05/21/1989)	34° (05/01/1996)
Jun.	81°	64.4°	4.3"	102° (06/24/1984)	info. unavailable
Jul.	88.4°	68°	3.9"	107° (07/30/1986)	54° (07/15/1990)
Aug.	93.1°	67°	3.1"	108° (08/01/1986)	50° (08/14/1967)
Sep.	86°	61.3°	4.7"	108° (09/02/1985)	36° (09/29/1967)
Oct.	76.4°	48.8°	4.3"	95° (10/02/1977)	25° (10/31/1993)
Nov.	64.8°	39.7°	4.5"	87° (11/06/1989)	11° (11/29/1976)
Dec.	54.9°	30.6°	4.1"	79° (12/15/1995)	2° (12/25/1983)

Yearly Average High 73.8°
Yearly Average Low 48.5°
Yearly Average Precipitation 51.9"

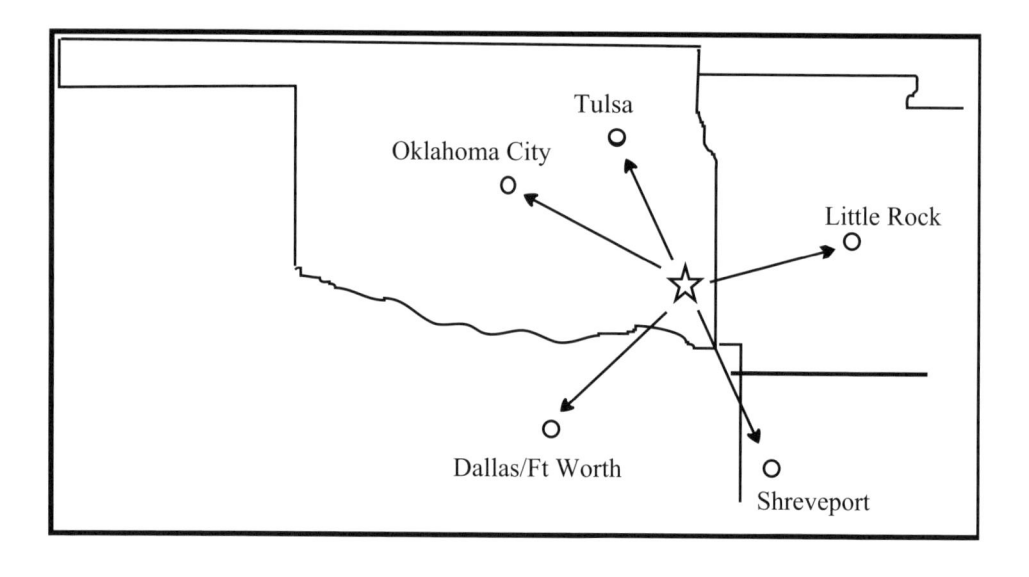

Where is Beavers Bend Resort Park located?

Beavers Bend Resort Park is tucked away in the extreme southeastern corner of Oklahoma. Because of its location it just might be the "best kept secret" of Oklahoma. In fact, of the more than 450,000 visitors to the park each year, far more are from the state of Texas than Oklahoma. Although many feel the Park is just too far away to travel to it's really centrally located, within three to four hours driving time of six sizeable metropolitan areas.

Dallas/Ft. Worth Area..........................4 hours
Shreveport..4 hours
Oklahoma City ....4 hours
Tulsa.. 3 ½ hours
Little Rock...3 hours

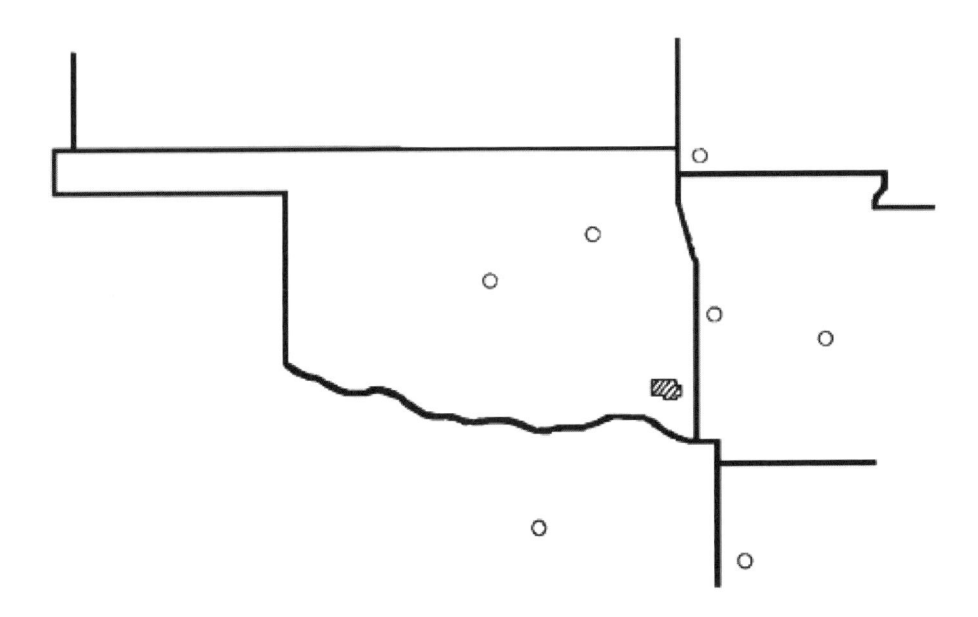

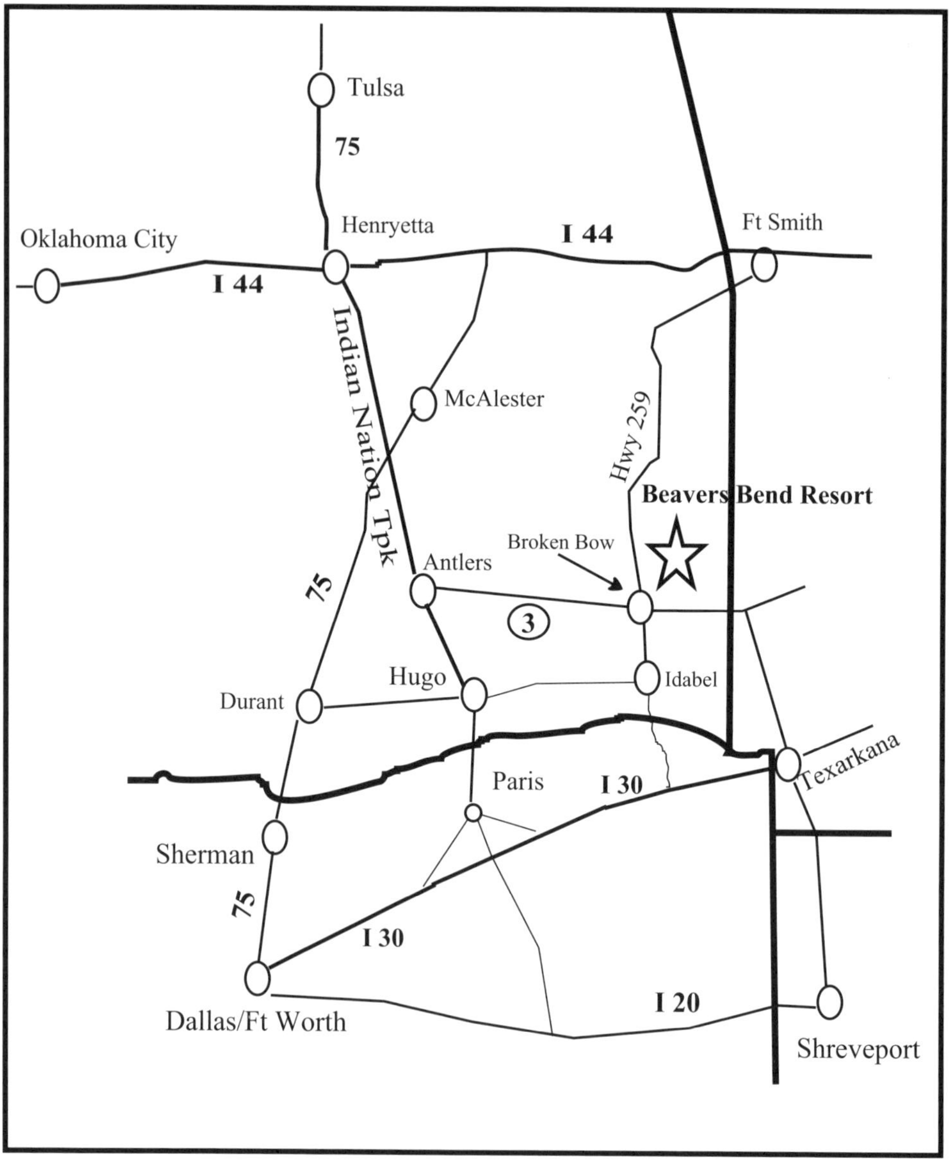
Tulsa
75
Oklahoma City
Henryetta
I 44
I 44
Ft Smith
Indian Nation Tpk
McAlester
Hwy 259
Beavers Bend Resort
Broken Bow
Antlers
75
3
Hugo
Idabel
Durant
Paris
I 30
Texarkana
Sherman
75
I 30
I 20
Dallas/Ft Worth
Shreveport

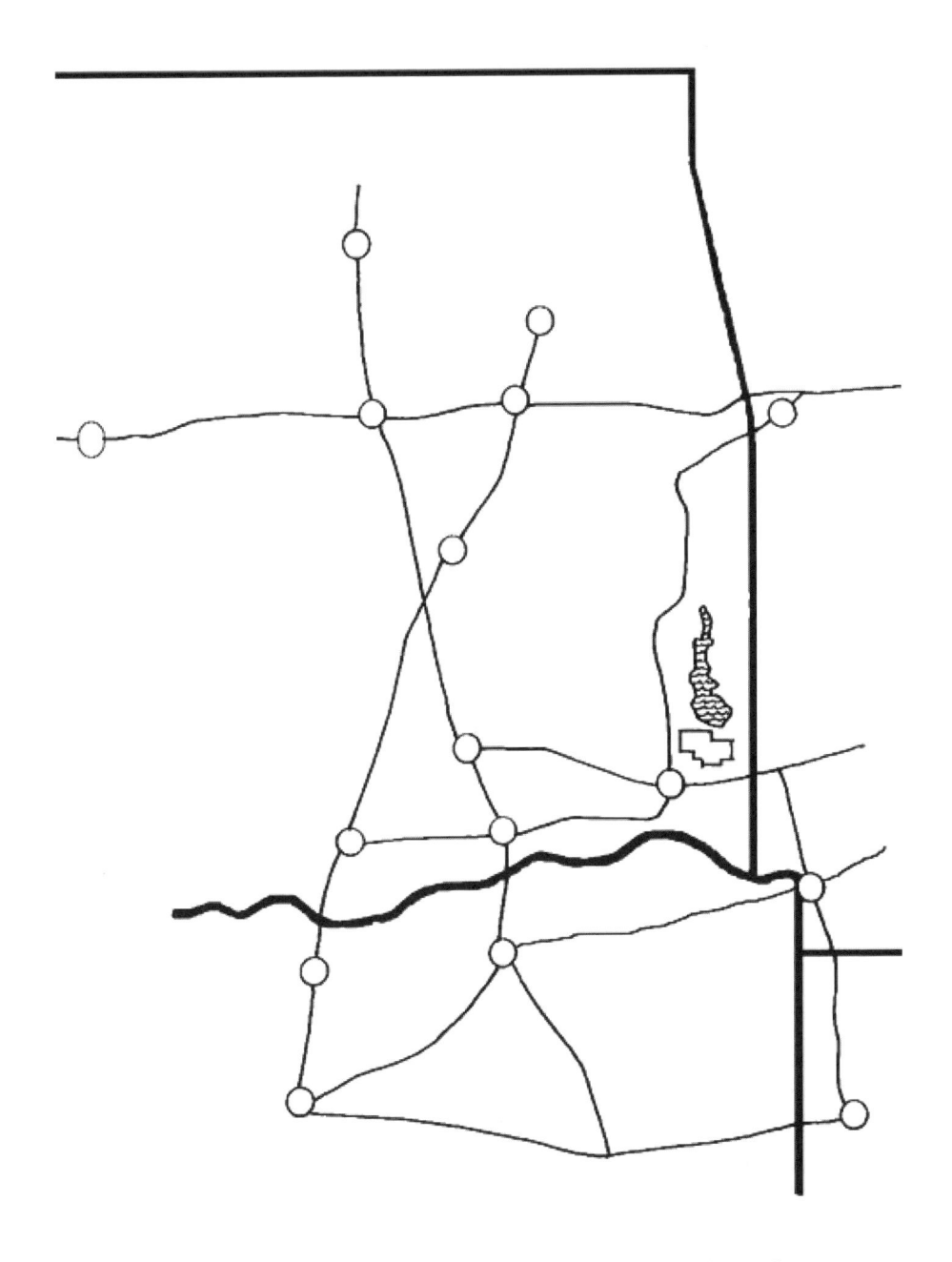

Good roads are also a plus. Interstate 30 is located south of the Park, Interstate 40 is north of the Park and Oklahoma's Indian Nation Turnpike is located west of the Park. All three major roads are within one to one-and-a-half hours driving time of the Park entrance. Although the roads to the Park from the major highways are two-lane they are well maintained, have good shoulders and are as straight and level as you can expect in this rural, forested area known as "The Little Smokies".

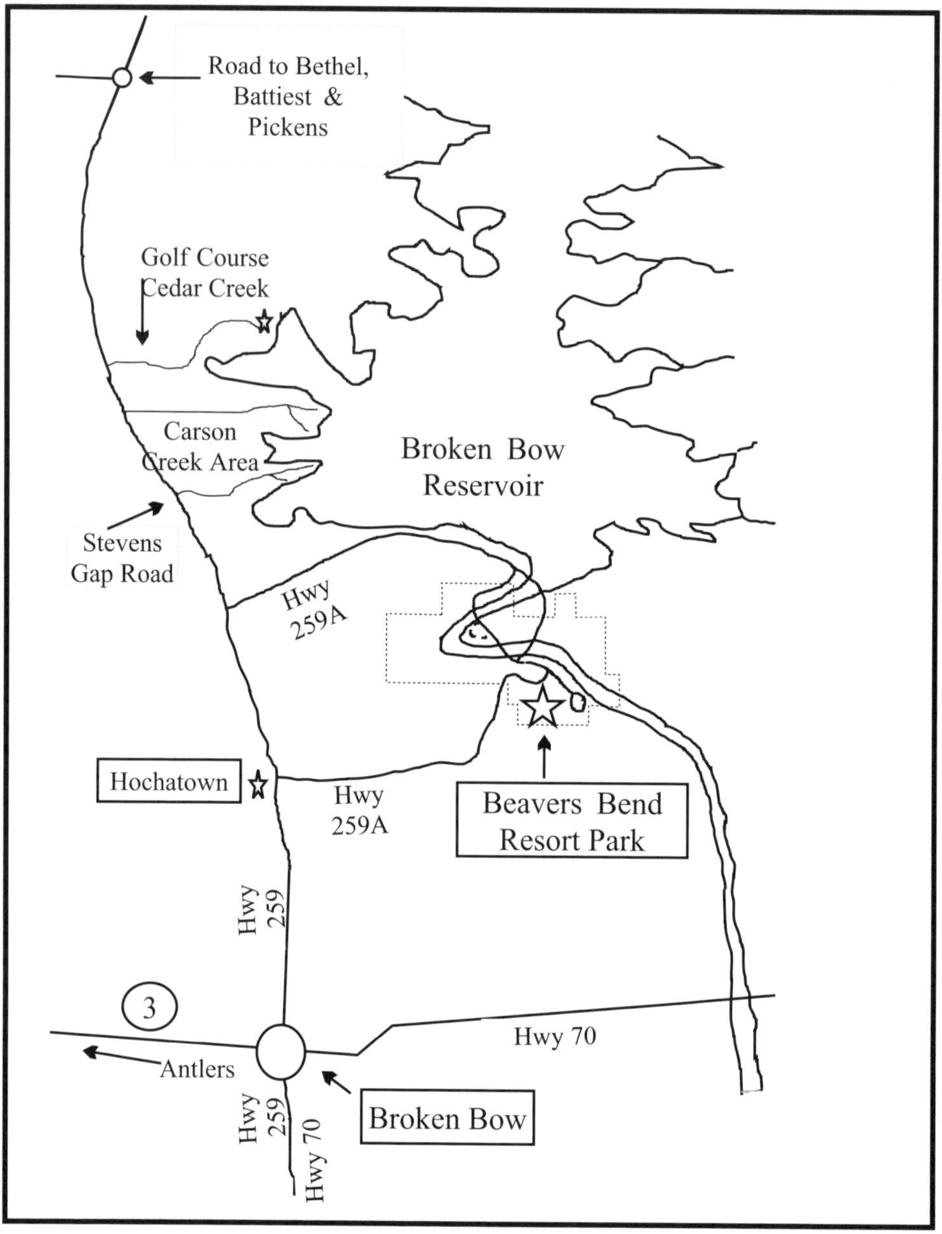
Road to Bethel,
Battiest &
Pickens
Golf Course
Cedar Creek
Carson
Creek Area
Broken Bow
Reservoir
Stevens
Gap Road
Hwy
259A
Hochatown
Hwy
259A
Beavers Bend
Resort Park
Hwy
259
3
Hwy 70
Antlers
Broken Bow
Hwy
259
Hwy 70

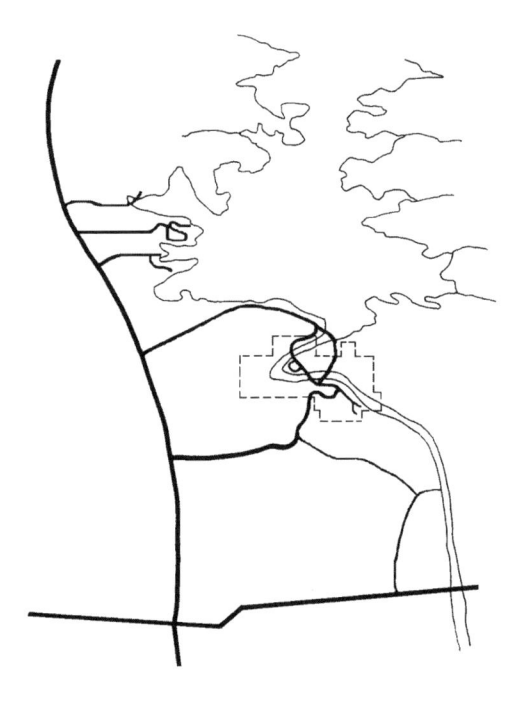

The Park is located seven miles north of Broken Bow, Oklahoma on Hwy 259. After traveling eight miles look for the sign "Beavers Bend Resort Park" and turn right onto Hwy 259A. This road winds five miles through the Ouachita (Wash-it-ta) National Forest as you enter the Park's main activity area to your right is the Oklahoma Forest Heritage Center. The Reservation Office, Information Center, Gift Shop and the Oklahoma Forest Heritage Center Museum are located here.

Hwy 259A circles through the Park and reconnects with Hwy 259.

Park History

The Beavers Bend Resort Park area has a rich and interesting history starting as far back as 130 million years ago when recently discovered new species of dinosaurs roamed the area.

The Mountain Fork River that flows through Beavers Bend Resort Area yielded the remains of an ancrocanthosaurus atokensis, a meat eating dinosaur from the early-mid Cretaceous Period, about 110 million years ago. At forty feet long it rivaled the more famous Tyrannosaurus Rex in size, although "Acro" is about 40 million years older. The Mountain Fork find, dubbed "Fran," turned out to be the most complete specimen of Acroanthosaurus found to date. The original fossil remains were purchased by the North Carolina Museum of Natural Sciences in Raleigh. A cast of the reconstructed dinosaur's skeleton is displayed at the Museum of the Red River in Idabel, twenty miles south of Beavers Bend. It's believed that more dinosaur bones are just waiting to be discovered in this same location southwest of Broken Bow.

Early nomad tribes passed through this area using it as part of their hunting territory as early as 5000 BC. More recent Indian tribes including the Choctaws, Quapaw, Osage, Shawnee, Comanche and Kiowa lived in this area beginning in the 1820's when after signing a series of treaties with the Federal Government agreed to relocate here. Southeastern Oklahoma at that time was rich in wildlife; bison, deer, bear, raccoon, fox beaver and otter are just some of the animals that where hunted and trapped and the area rivers were teeming with catfish, gar, bass, sunfish, and eel.

This park in the southeast corner of Oklahoma in the south-central Ouachita Mountains was officially named after John T. Beavers, a settler who had received the land as part of his 1,500 acre Choctaw Indian allotment. A portion of the Beaver Creek Trail was the original road to John T. Beaver's home site. A concrete slab is all that remains of one of his family's early homes. In 1930 he sold the land to the Dierk's Choctaw Lumber Company for $10,000. This company later sold the land to local merchants who with the help of the Oklahoma State Planning and Resources Board created Beavers Bend State Park in 1937.

The Civilian Conservation Corps (CCC) worked in the area in the late 1930's and early 1940's developing the park by building roads, cabins, campgrounds, residences and a bathhouse for the swimming area. The Works Progress Authority (WPA) at the same time built a low water dam across the Mountain Fork River near the southwestern corner of the park, creating a long, narrow lake ideal for swimming and boating. (The old swimming area is directly behind the Nature Center.) Originally the park consisted of approximately 1300 acres containing between 13 to 17 rental cabins, a cabin/park office building, one campground, the bathhouse and a swimming beach.

Creation of Broken Bow Lake was authorized by the 1958 and 1967 Flood Control Acts. The Lake was designed and built under the supervision of the Department of the Army Tulsa District Corps of Engineers. Construction began November 1961 and completed in October 1969.

Today Beavers Bend Resort Park encompassing over 14,240 water acres and 3,482 park land acres of pine and hardwood forest, and hilly terrain is affectionately referred to as Oklahoma's "Little Smokies".

South entrance to the Park
from Hwy 259 North

Forest Heritage Center,
Gift Shop, Cabin Reservation Center

Beavers Bend Nature Center

Beavers Bend Swimming Area

16

Trail Head Sign for the
Pine Ridge Nature Trail

Trail Head Sign for the
David Boren Hiking Trail

Places To Stay In The Park

Finding a place to stay in the Broken Bow area is not a problem. For those that like to get close to nature and really rough it, there are a number of tent sites available at Beavers Bend Resort Park which includes Beavers Bend State Park, as well as what is now called the Stevens Gap and Carson Creek Areas. For those that like to get close to nature but like the comforts of home they will find that all three areas have a good number of prepared RV sites with water, electric, and sewer. No reservations are taken, they are all on first-come availability.

Other choices for those that want more conventional lodging are the Lakeview Lodge overlooking Broken Bow Lake, and cabins in Beavers Bend Resort Park and numerous private cabins located a short distance from Beavers Bend Resort Park.

Within Beavers Bend Resort Park

Tent Camping:

Beavers Bend State Park
6 miles north of Broken Bow on Hwy 259N, turn right on Hwy 259A to Park

56 tent sites - $ 8.00 per day, water and comfort station w/showers located nearby. No reservations taken. You will pay a Camp Host at the campsite.

These sites are centrally located near many of the central activity areas. Nature center, gift shop, tennis courts, museum, canoeing, swimming, hiking, and other activities are within walking distance or just a short drive.

Beavers Bend Resort Park (Stevens Gap Area)
Located 10 miles from Broken Bow on Hwy 259N, turn right on Stevens Gap Road.

150 tent sites - $ 8.00 per day, water and comfort station w/showers located nearby. No reservations taken. You will pay a Camp Host at the campsite.

If your interest is fishing, swimming and motorized water sports you should check out this camping area. Multi-use hiking and mountain bike trails pass by Camping Area "1". The Beavers Bend Marina is located just down the road.

Beavers Bend Resort Park (Carson Creek Area)
Located 12 miles from Broken Bow on Hwy 259N, turn right on Carson Creek Road.

There are a number of primitive tent sites in this area. Water and comfort station w/showers is located nearby. No reservations taken, select your camp area and pay a Camp Host at the campsite.

Those interested in fishing, swimming and motorized water sports should check out this camping area. A multi-use hiking and mountain bike trail is on the south side of the road. Look for a Trail Head Sign to find where the tail begins.

RV Camping:

Beavers Bend State Park
6 miles north of Broken Bow on Hwy 259N, turn right on Hwy 259A to the Park.

110 RV sites with water and electric. Tent campers are welcome in these areas also. 2 group picnic shelters available. Reservations are required.

No individual reservations are taken, they are all on first-come availability. Large groups however can still reserve camp sites. Find the campsite you want, payment is made to a Camp Host or Ranger.
This is a very popular park so there are no guarantees that sites will be available. Come early and have a back-up plan. The Stevens Gap and Carson Creek Areas located a short distance away have 71 RV sites and even more primitive camp areas.

Beavers Bend Resort Park (Stevens Gap Area)
Located 10 miles from Broken Bow on Hwy 259N, turn right on Stevens Gap Road.

50 RV sites with water and electric.
21 RV sites with water, electric and sewer.
2 group picnic shelters available. Reservations are required.

No individual reservations are taken, they are all on first-come availability. Find the campsite you want, payment is made to a Camp Host or Ranger. This is also a very popular area to camp so come early and have a back-up plan in case these sites are full.

Beavers Bend Resort Park (Carson Creek Area)
Located 12 miles from Broken Bow on Hwy 259N, turn right on Carson Creek Road. 25 RV sites with water and electric, a dump station is close-by.

No individual reservations are taken, they are all on first-come availability. Find the campsite you want, payment is made to a Camp Host or Ranger. This is also a very popular area to camp so come early and have a back-up plan in case these sites are full.

Beavers Bend Resort Park Lodge and Cabins:

Lakeview Lodge
Located 10 miles from Broken Bow on Hwy 259N, turn right on Stevens Gap Road.
Lodge Reservations 1 (800) 435-5514
www.beaversbend.com
Accommodations:
36 rooms and 4 suites, 1 large meeting room.
Depending on the season, reservations should be made six months to one year in advance. The Lakeview Lodge is a modern but rustic looking structure with a beautiful view overlooking Beavers Bend Lake. The Lodge was designed so that every room would have a spectacular view of the lake. Beavers Bend Marina is located just down the road.

Park Cabins
6 miles north of Broken Bow on Hwy 259N, turn right on Hwy 259A to the Park. Check in at the reservation desk located in the Forest Heritage Center.
Cabin reservations: 1 (580) 494-6300
www.beaversbend.com
Accommodations:
48 cabins, sleeping 2, 4 or 6 guests.
1 handicapped accessible cabin.
All have small kitchens and are set up for light housekeeping. Some have indoor fireplaces, all have outdoor fire pits. Pets are welcomed. Depending on the season, reservations should be made six months to one year in advance. Cabins are located in several areas within the park. Some are located along the Mountain Fork River while others are located in isolated cul-de-sacs surrounded by 100 foot native Pine trees.

Don't get discouraged if there are no cabins available. Just outside the park are numerous modern rustic looking private cabins (some with hot tubs) within easy driving distance.

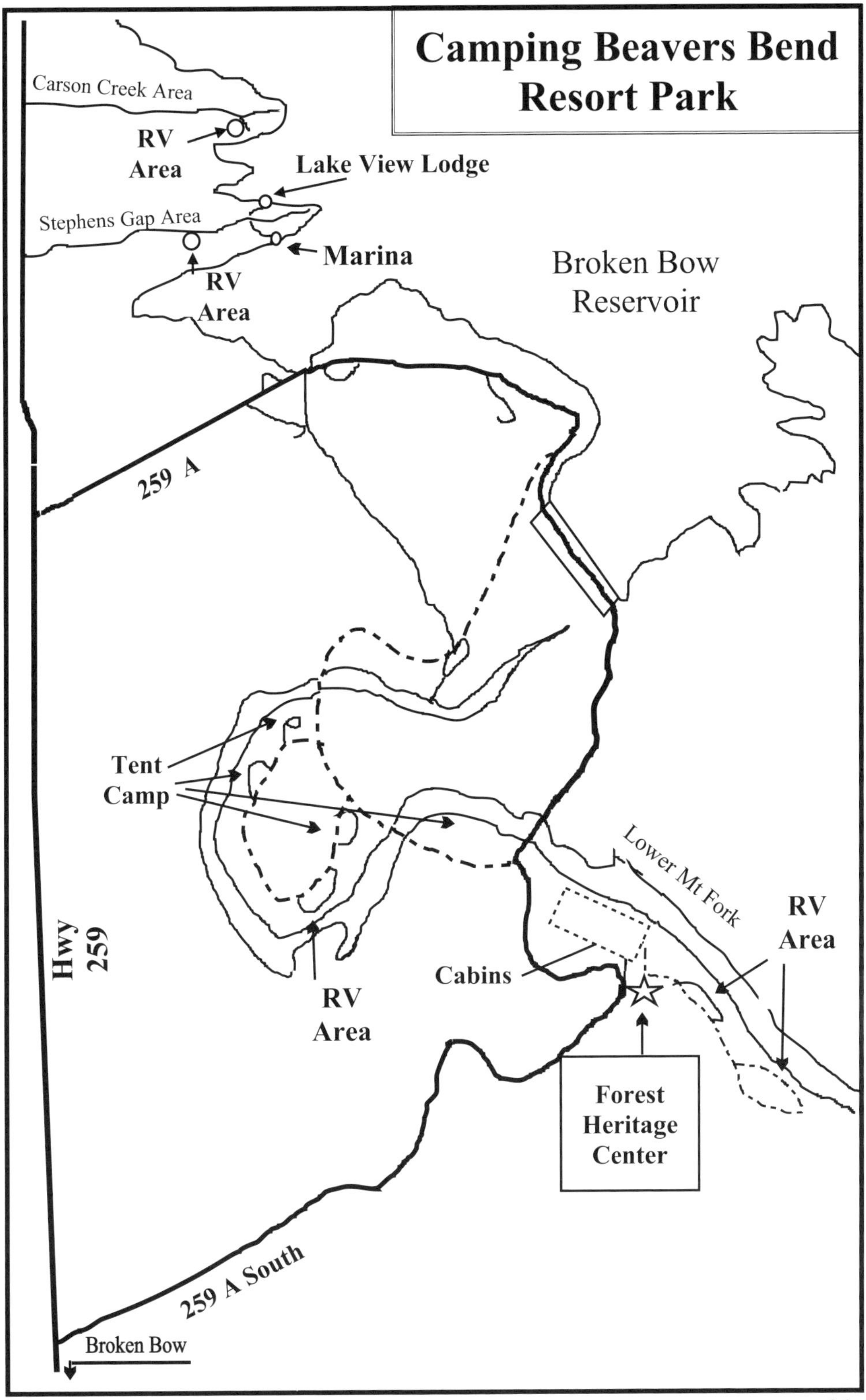
Camping Beavers Bend Resort Park
Carson Creek Area
RV Area
Lake View Lodge
Stephens Gap Area
Marina
RV Area
Broken Bow Reservoir
259 A
Tent Camp
Lower Mt Fork
RV Area
Cabins
RV Area
Hwy 259
Forest Heritage Center
259 A South
Broken Bow

Places To Stay Outside Beavers Bend Resort Park

Cabin accommodations range from outdoor rustic to more luxurious than you would find at a five star resort. To find the cabin just right for you, read the following cabin descriptions and then go to the web sites of the ones that interest you. Look at the detailed description and pictures before making your final selection.

*1   A to Z Guest Ranch
*2   Beavers Bend Getaways
*3   Broken Bow Lake Cabins
*4   Cabin In The Woods
 5   Contentment Cottages
*6   Crooked River Cabins
*7   East Fork Getaway
*8   Heartpine Hollow Retreats
 9   Hickory Hill Cabins
*10 Hochatown Junction Resort
 11 Kiamichi Country Cabins
 12 Last Resort Cabins
*13 Ponderosa Cabins
 14 Reuben's Rest Bed and Breakfast
*15 River's Bend Resort
*16 River's Edge Cottages
 17 Sleepy Hollow
*18 Three Oaks Cabins
*19 Timberwolf Cabins
 20 Tomichi Cabins
*21 Tree Top View Cabins
*22 Whip-Poor-Will Resort
*23 Wilderness Lakefront Resort

*Featured cabins with descriptions

23

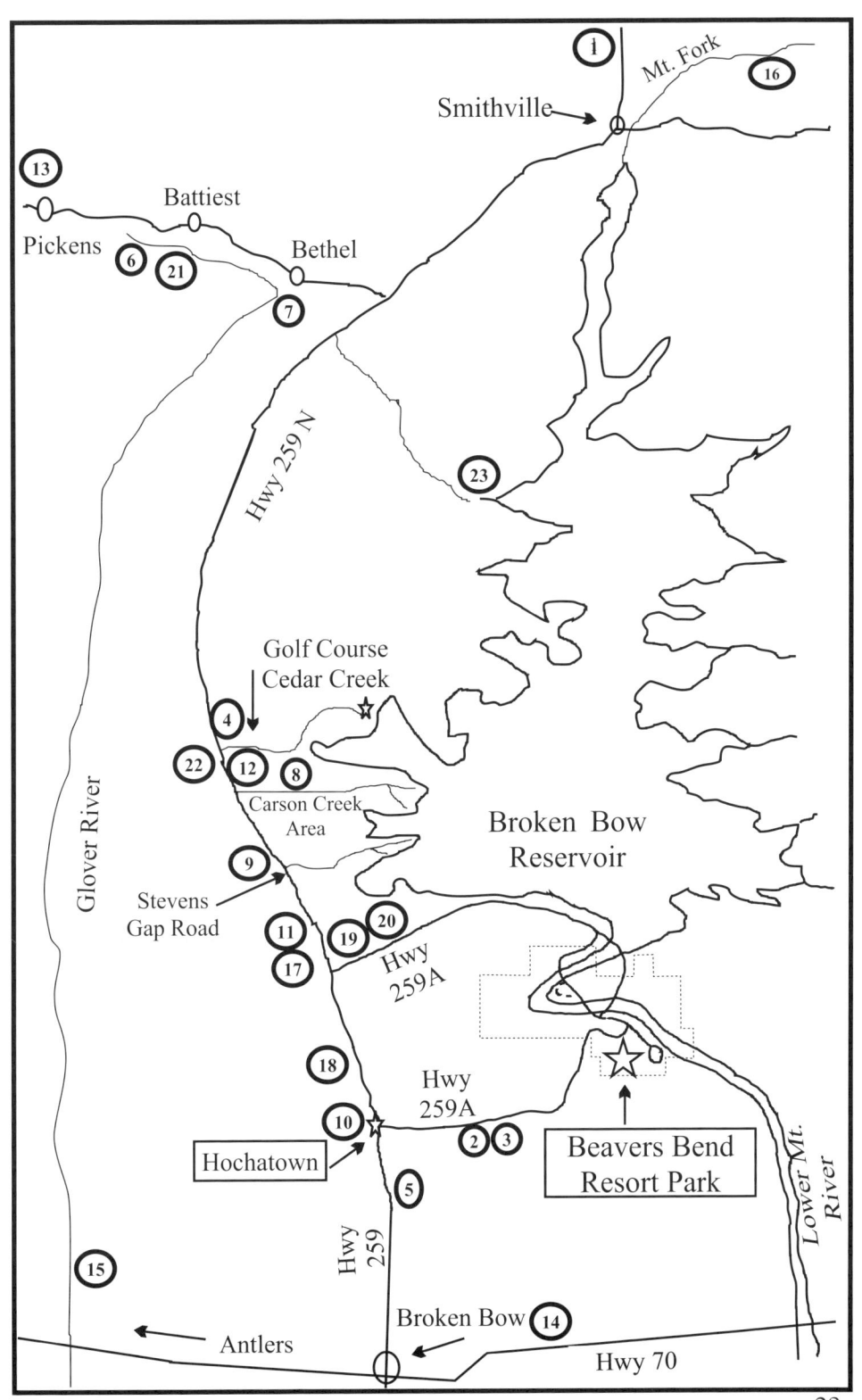

Featured Cabins

1) A to Z Guest Ranch
North of Smithville
(580) 244-3729
atozguestranch.com

If you want to experience the old west, check out A to Z Guest Ranch located north of Smithville on Hwy 259. You can't get closer to wilderness in Oklahoma than here. They are situated next to 725,000 acres of Department of Wildlife Land for you to explore on horse back or ATV. They also have over 1437 acres of private land to ride on which does not require a permit. The owners, Andy and Zondra Lewis, can also provide you with a map with over 150 miles of marked equestrian trails to explore.

Bring your own horse and organize your own private trail ride or join one of our organized trail rides. Don't have a horse? They have ten rental horses to choose from to ride on a guided trail ride. If you want to take a trail ride that's more than just going around in a circle this is the place for you! If your interest is ATVing, explore on your own or take a guided ATV ride (you must provide your own ATV).

A to Z Guest Ranch has four cabins to choose from. The largest is a beautiful log cabin which will accommodate up to 17 guests. This cabin has two bedrooms on the first floor which are furnished with one queen and one full size bed in each. In the open loft area you'll find five twin and two full size beds. The open floor plan for the living room and fully equipped kitchen makes a nice social gathering area for guests.

They also have 27 RV sites with water and electric hookups. There are fire rings and picnic tables available in each of the sites. You have a choice of a campsite with outside corrals or one with covered stalls for your horse. A dump station is also located nearby for your convenience.
For our camping guests only - Dogs are allowed in the campsites ONLY if the owner keeps them on a leash at all times. The owner MUST clean up after their dogs. We can not allow barking dogs in our camp!

2) Beavers Bend Getaways
Broken Bow Lake/Beavers Bend Area
(580) 494-6116
www.BeaversBendGetaways.com

Deep in the mountains of Southeastern Oklahoma is a mountain lake surrounded by national forests, state parks, clear running streams and the kind of solitude that has to be experienced to be truly appreciated. Beavers Bend Getaways is a collection of privately owned top-of-the-line cabins offering modern conveniences in comfortable settings, and just minutes from outdoor fun!
The best part is this wonderful outdoor experience is that it's just a few hours drive from the Dallas - Fort Worth area, Shreveport, Tulsa, and Oklahoma City! Within 3 to 4 hours of leaving the congested big city rat race you'll be pulling off the freeway and begin climbing into the Kiamichi mountains, headed for Broken Bow Lake and the Beavers Bend State Park area.
All of these gorgeous cabins offer large hot tubs and fireplaces; many offer game rooms, bikes, and seclusion. These upscale accommodations offer the complete package--first class quality, amenities galore, and atmosphere--everything you need for a great multi-couple retreat, family outing, or romantic getaway.
Each of these cabins are located within a five minute drive from both scenic Broken Bow Lake and Beavers Bend State Park. Nearby activities include hiking, biking, canoeing, swimming, trout fishing, lake fishing, boat and jet ski rentals, horseback riding, museums, playgrounds, golf, putt-putt golf, and go-carts.
Call Joe or Lindy Silk at (580) 494-6116 to book your Beavers Bend Getaway. Drive-by business welcome.

3) Broken Bow Lake Cabins
9 miles N Hwy 259
(580) 286-4471
www.brokenbowlakecabins.com

Broken Bow Lake Cabins offers 20 privately-owned cabins, all located within minutes from Beavers Bend Resort Park, Broken Bow Lake, fly fishing, river floats, hiking, and many other outdoor activities. Because the cabins are situated throughout the Beavers Bend Area and each is very unique, check out Broken Bow Lake Cabins Web Site for locations and detailed descriptions.
Cabins range from 600 to 3000 square feet in size and can comfortably sleep from four to eleven people. Each has its own very secluded location among the pines. Most cabins have a deck, perfect for grilling or barbequing and new hot tubs. Cabins also have fireplaces and an outdoor fire pit where kids can roast their marshmallows. Wood is complimentary for fireplaces and fire pits. All cabins have a strict no pet and no smoking policy.

4) Cabin In The Woods
12 miles N Hwy 259
(580) 286-8687 or (580) 494-7370
www.hochatownusa.com

Cabin-in-the-Woods is only a five minute drive from Cedar Creek Golf Course, Beaver's Bend State Park and Broken Bow Lake and can accommodate up to six guests but is also perfect for a couple looking for a weekend getaway. To better accommodate all of our guests we ask that you please do not bring pets or smoke inside the cabin. The cabin includes one bedroom with a full bath and another half bath, central heat and air, cable TV with movie channels, a full size stove and refrigerator, king size bed and day bed, queen sleeper sofa, two foldaway cots, all linens, gas grill, coffee pot and kitchen equipment provided. The back deck or front porch is a great place to kick back and relax. There is a firepit outside for that marshmallow roast and plenty of parking for the boat. Cabin is managed by the owner, very clean and caters to the family who wants to have a nice vacation without spending a lot of money. Prices range from $80 to $120 night. Discounts for seniors and stays of four nights or over.

6) Crooked River Cabins
P.O. Box 10 Battiest, OK 7472
33 miles N Hwy 259
(580) 241-5709
www.crookedrivercabins.com

Escape to Southeast Oklahoma's Glover River and enjoy our Luxury Cabins in Beavers Bend Country. These luxury cabins are situated on a bluff overlooking the Glover River, the last free flowing stream in Oklahoma! Crooked River Cabins offer a private wilderness experience but with luxury amenities you will not find anywhere else. All cabins include, private outdoor hot tub, VCR/DVD, satellite TV, floor to ceiling windows and French doors, covered decks with river views and extra large covered patios with grills and picnic tables. The cabins are completely stocked with everything you will need to enjoy your stay except for your food and your family or that special someone! All cabins have a strict no pet and no smoking allowed policy. Pedal boats are now available to rent for kids (of all ages!) to use on the beautiful stretch of the Glover River near our cabins. Interested in guided hunting, fishing, canoeing and ATV tours, Crooked River Cabins can help you arrange professionally guided tours for your party. Our expert guides can take you on canoeing or inner tube tours of the Glover River. Our fishing tours cover the Glover, Little River and Mountain Fork and can also be done with inner tubes. Our guided hunting trips will lead you to wild hogs, deer and turkey (in season.) Crooked River Cabins is also an ATV rider's paradise. You are welcome to bring your ATV's and you can access 450,000 acres directly from your cabin.

7) East Fork Getaway
25 miles N Hwy 259
(580) 241-5393
www.eastforkgetaway.com

East Fork Getaway's secluded country cottage is located on the east fork of the Glover River near Beavers Bend Resort Park and Broken Bow Lake. It offers the combination of comfortable lodging big enough for large groups and access to a wild outdoor adventure paradise in Southeast Oklahoma's McCurtain County. The country cottage is a large, two story cottage, complete with four separate bedrooms. Because of its ample size it is the perfect Oklahoma vacation destination for large groups, family reunions or a corporate retreat. Each of the four bedrooms offer a queen bed. There are two separate bathrooms; one featuring a whirlpool spa bath and the other with a walk-in shower. The cottage has a large, open plan kitchen. It's just right for preparing meals for large groups and comes equipped with a full size refrigerator, stove, microwave oven and coffee maker. Of course all of your utensils, dishes, glasses, coffee mugs and cookware are provided. The cottage also has a full sized washer and dryer which might come in handy for extended stays. The cottage also has a gas log fireplace, satellite TV and a romantic outdoor hot tub nestled in its own cozy gazebo.

8) Heartpine Hollow Retreats
10 miles N Hwy 259
(580) 241-7895
www.southeastokcabins.com

Is it time for a little R & R? If so, Heartpine Hollow Retreats might be the place for you. Whatever you are looking for, whether it's the peace and quiet that our beautiful and luxurious cabins offer or if you are looking for more to occupy your time, you can visit the numerous attractions located within minutes of our retreat. Attractions include the beautiful Beavers Bend State Park, Broken Bow Lake and Cedar Creek Golf Course. Kids might be interested in riding the go-carts, playing miniature golf or going canoeing down the breathtaking Mountain Fork River. And of course, don't forget to check out the hiking and ATV Trails. Heartpine Hollow Retreat has six new cabins to choose from. Depending on the cabin they can accommodate from 6 to 10 people. They have one called the Honeymoon Cabin, which is just right for a couple or small family. All come equipped with a full modern kitchen with dishwasher, microwave, toaster, and coffee maker. Included are dishes, cookware, cooking and grilling utensils. Each comes with linens and towels. The cabins also come with TV/DVD player with DVDs and a washer/dryer. Several cabins come with either Jacuzzi or hot tubs.

10) Hochatown Junction Resort
7 miles N Hwy 259
Office located in The Cedar Chest
(580) 494-6521 or 1-800-550-6521
www.hochatownjunction.com

Hochatown Junction Resort, located 7 miles north of Broken Bow across from the 259A turn off to Beavers Bend Resort Park, has a large selection of cabins (60) to choose from. Depending on your needs and the size of your party, your choices range from efficiency cabins to vacation homes. Your choices include one, two, three and four bedroom cabins that can accommodate up to 9 people. Cabins include either a charcoal or propane gas grill. Most cabins have full kitchens equipped with a full-size refrigerator, a range and oven, a microwave, a coffee maker, a toaster/toaster oven and a variety of pots and pans, dishware, glassware and flatware. A number of cabins have fireplaces, washer/dryer, dishwasher and either a Jacuzzi or hot tub. A few cabins have kitchenettes equipped with a small refrigerator, a microwave, and a coffee maker. The cabins also include color TVs with VCRs, DVDs, cable or satellite reception. Only a very few cabins have telephone connections. The cabin rental office is open between 9 AM and 5 PM Monday through Thursday. Friday office hours are 9 AM to 6 PM. Saturday office hours are 9 AM to 3 PM. Office hours on Sunday are 10 AM to noon. All cabins are "non-smoking" and "no pets". Linens are provided in the cabins.

13) Ponderosa Cabins
203 East Baggs Lane
Pickens, OK 74752
(580) 241-5555 or 5453
www.ponderosacabinsok.com

Ponderosa Cabins, located north of Beavers Bend and overlooking Silver Creek is a paradise location for horseback riders and 4-wheeler enthusiasts. Located in the heart of the Three Rivers Wild Management Area and Quachita National Forest; it's like having a 800,000 acre backyard! If your interest is guided wild hog or turkey hunts this is your place. 4-wheeler and ATV tours (need to provide your own) and guided horse rides (horses available) can also be arranged if that's your interest. Land use permits, hunting and fishing licenses can also be purchased on site. There are three one-bedroom cabins to choose from, each decorated in a different theme (western, wildlife or light house) all come with private bedroom, full bath, double futon in the living room, and linens are provided.

15) River's Bend Resort
Glover River
(580) 584-3321 Mon-Fri 8AM - 5 PM
(580) 420-3040 Nights and Weekends
Fax (580) 584-3237
www.riversbendresort.com
charlette@direcway.com

River's Bend Resort is an isolated group of luxury vacation rentals nestled along the Glover River and is a refuge from the hustle and bustle of life. These are not your typical rustic country cabins. The three cottages are designed with a contemporary flair and luxury furnishings usually found only in the great resorts of Colorado and California.

Each cabin has leather sofas, satellite television with surround sound and DVD player. They also have a large dining room table, a kitchen that is fully stocked with utensils and flatware and a full range of premium appliances including dishwasher, microwave and water purifier. Each cottage has an extensive deck overlooking the Glover River equipped with gas grills. The deck is the perfect spot in the early morning hours to experience native birds, deer, raccoons and other wildlife as they start their day.

Bathrooms are outfitted with hydrotherapy Pearl Apoge Showers, to the tune of $10,000 each, with full body spray and pulsating Grohe showerheads. Back and foot massagers double as whirlpool/Jacuzzi jets so the unit may be used as a shower or a relaxing whirlpool bath.

The Glover River is the last wild free flowing river in Oklahoma and is known for its elusive small mouth bass fishing. Each cottage at River's Bend Resort has its own canoe that is always available.

16) Rivers Edge Cottages
25 miles North of Beavers Bend
(580) 244-7296
www.RiversEdgeCottages.com

The River's Edge is a peaceful resort on the banks of the upper Mountain Fork River in northern McCurtain County. It is located 15 minutes east of Smithville, which is 25 miles north of the Beavers Bend and Broken Bow Lake areas. The resort is situated on 300 acres of private land and is surrounded by timberlands that are all public access. With more than 2 miles of river front, Rivers Edge has plenty of wilderness hiking and wandering to do.
Your cabin will include a pair of mountain bikes and canoes are ready for you at the river when you arrive. With fireplaces, jacuzzis for two, and all the amenities you could ask for, these cabins are ideal accommodations for couples seeking to rekindle the fires of romance and perfect for families looking to build memories that will last a lifetime. River's Edge Cottages have six cabins to choose from ranging in style from log cabins to mountain top chalets overlooking the Mountain Fork and the surrounding scenic, Kiamichi Mountains. The selection includes cabins built strictly for romance, 2 BR cabins great for families, and larger multi-family accommodations that include 3BR's, pool and foosball tables, large hot tubs, and incredible views. All cabins are completely furnished and include firewood, charcoal grills, canoes, and bikes.
Call Tim and Suzy Knapp at 580-244-7296 to book your riverside retreat today. Reservations only.

18) Three Oaks, Crooked Oaks Cabins, Mustang,
Fishin' Fever and Safari Cabins
1 mile from Beavers Bend State Park
1-866-4ok-mtns (1-866-465-6867) or (580) 494-6201
www.4okmtns.com

These affordable cabins are great for families on a budget and like a rustic look. All cabins are centrally located to the main attractions within the Beavers Bend area. The Three Oaks Cabins are located north of the main park entrance and are nearer to Broken Bow Lake. Your cabin choices include one room studio with queen size beds and queen sleeper sofas, one bedroom with queen size bed and sleeper sofa, and one to four bedroom cabins that sleep 6 -12 people. The Fishin' Fever and Safari Cabins are duplex cabins with an 8' breezeway and are ideal for two couples vacationing together or enough privacy for individual guests. Small house-trained pets are allowed in these duplex cabins. All cabins have fully equipped kitchens, (including coffee and condiments) air conditioning and several have either log or gas fireplaces, cable tv and vcrs, decks, bbq grills, lawn furniture, picnic tables, and fire circles (wood furnished). The Crooked Oaks Cabins have a pond nearby stocked with fish.

19) Timberwolf Cabins
HC75 Box 360, Broken Bow, OK 74728
12 miles N Hwy 259
(580) 494-6363
www.timberwolfcabins.com

Timberwolf Cabins are located just 3 miles from the nearest boat dock, 2 miles from a convenience store, 2 miles to restaurants and within 3 miles of the Carson Creek 18 hole golf course. Easy pull-in and pull-out parking makes these cabins attractive to vehicles carrying ATVs. You have a choice of cabins that can accommodate 4 to 8 people. The new spacious 576 square foot one bedroom cabin has a full kitchen, satellite TV, 150 channels, VCR, charcoal grills, picnic tables and camp fire area. The largest cabin also has a living area fireplace and a vaulted ceiling with a loft bedroom. A 5 person hot tub in a protected gazebo sits between the two cabins. Both cabins are newly built in a modern rustic décor. No smoking or pets allowed in cabins.
Look for the Timber Wolf Cabins sign on the west side of Hwy 259 about four miles north of the north Park entrance.

21) Tree Top View Cabins
1 Mile South of Battiest
(580) 241-5599 or Fax (580) 241-5356
cabins@pine-net.com
www.treetopviewcabins.com

Feel the stress melt away as you sit on the large deck watching the hummingbirds at the feeder just a few feet from you and the soft whisper of the Glover River just below. You're in one of Tree Top View's unique cabins that are nestled deep in the woods of Southeastern Oklahoma. You're surrounded by a beautiful wilderness that has been left in its natural state. Once you are fully rested you may want to explore the breathtaking surroundings. You can canoe down the Glover River, play on the rustic playground, go hiking, biking, fishing, or horseback riding and visiting the new swing bridge is a must!
Each cabin is modern with fully equipped kitchens and a full bath with towels. All sleep six with one queen, one double, and two twin beds, with linens furnished. Each one also has heating and air conditioning. All have a large deck overlooking the Glover River. Notify us in advance if you are interested in us providing horses for a guided trail ride.

22) Whip-Poor-Will Resort
12 miles N Hwy 259
(580) 494-6476
www.okresort.com

Conveniently located 12 miles north of Broken Bow, Oklahoma on Highway 259 across from the entrance to Cedar Creek Golf Course; Whip-Poor-Will Resort has 17 cabins of various sizes on 15 heavily wooded acres to accommodate couples, families and large groups. If you're looking for authentic log cabins decorated with a special touch that will take you back in time, check these cabins out. Most of the cabins have been recently remodeled or refurbished. Cabins range in size from their romantic, one room honeymoon cabin to several 1200 sq. ft. two and three bedroom cabins. All cabins are fully furnished and equipped with full kitchens, cable TV, and charcoal grills. They are also air-conditioned and heated; most cabins have fireplaces or wood burning stoves. There is also a large fishing pond and playground area for the kids, horseshoe pits and volleyball, and a gathering spot great for large groups. Another plus is the ample parking available for boats and ATV trailers. Whip-Poor-Will Resort is located very near to access into Ouachita National Forest and Three Rivers Wildlife Management Area for hunters and ATV enthusiasts.

23) Wilderness Lakefront Resort
HC 75 Box 308-10 Broken Bow
(580) 241-5304
www.lakefrontresort.com

Wilderness Lakefront Resort is located on the north end of the beautiful Broken Bow Lake in the Kiamichi Mountains. If you're looking for cabins located away from all the hustle and bustle so you can the enjoy peace and quiet of this beautiful wilderness area, these are the cabins you should check out. The rustic log cabins are set on 5 acres adjoining the McCurtain County Wilderness Area. The cabins blend into the surrounding forested area and remind you of what life was like a century ago. All cabins are rustic log cabin looking on the outside but totally new and modern on the inside. If you're looking for a secluded and relaxed atmosphere, this might be your place. All cabins come furnished with towels, linens, pots and pans, silverware, dishes, cooking utensils, paper towels, and salt and pepper. (All you need is food!) Each cabin has central heat and air and satellite TV. The gazebo/fire pit is centrally located between the cabins, and is great for grilling or just relaxing around the fire. An added bonus is the new swimming pool which offers fun, enjoyment, and relaxation for the whole family. A boat ramp is located only a ½ mile away and ATV trails are also accessible from the cabins. There is a nature trail that takes you down to the lake and canoes are also available for use. The cabins are located 12.5 miles north of Stevens Gap exit on US 259 North then 8 miles east on Sherwood Rd.

Things To Do Inside The Park

Beavers Bend Resort Park offers a wealth of activities to choose from. For those that like the traditional outdoor activities; hiking, mountain biking, canoeing, swimming, water skiing and fishing as well other activities, are close by. Other activities just a sort distance from your camping area or cabin include golfing, paddle boats, horseback riding, train rides, hay rides, tennis, and volleyball. For those that just want to relax in the solitude of Mother Nature they will have no problem finding a quiet, secluded area within the 14,000 acre park.

The Park hosts four popular and heavily attended arts and craft festivals: (For more information on the arts and craft festivals call The Forest Heritage Center (580) 494-6497)

Annual Spring Wood Art Exhibit (March–May) Features the wood art works of clubs or groups from across the nation. Groups have included; the Central Oklahoma Woodturners, the Northwest Coast Wood Artists, the Dallas Area Woodturners and Carvers from the Ozarks.

Kiamichi Owa-Chito "Festival of the Forest" and Art Show (June) Kiamichi Owa-Chito is from the Choctaw Indian Tribe and means a "coming together" of the people. The mid-summer festival is an annual event to acquaint the people of Oklahoma and surrounding states and the world with the beauty, heritage, industry and progress associated with Kiamichi County. Events and activities include: forestry competition, art show, photography show, talent contest, Little Miss Owa Chito, horseshoes, canoe races, golf tournament, archery competition, 5-K run, children's events, backwoods venue, and plenty of arts, crafts and food vendors.

Masters Wood Art Exhibit (September–October) Features the works of some of the finest individual wood turners, carvers and sculptors from across the nation.

The Folk Festival and Craft Show (November) is held over a three day period the 2nd weekend in November bringing in about 17,000 visitors to southeastern Oklahoma each year. It features turn-of-the-century authentic demonstrations, arts, food, and folk music. Almost 70 exhibitors and vendors will feature crafts and skills like candle making, woodturning, lye soap making, knife making and quilting. Herbalists will share their knowledge. Instrument makers will exhibit their work. Quilters will show their best.

It also includes a petting zoo for kids and a children's activity area where kids have an opportunity to create a puppet show with their imagination and their very own handmade paper puppets. Food vendors will have a wide variety of food for your eating pleasure.

Things To Do Inside The Park

  1   Beavers Bend Canoe Rental

  2   Beavers Bend Depot

*3   Beavers Bend Fly Shop

*4   Beavers Bend Gift Shop

*   Beavers Bend Marina (Located in Stephens Gap Area)

*5   Beavers Bend Nature Center

  6   Beavers Bend Swimming Area

  7   Beavers Bend Water Park And Miniature Golf

  8   Children's Playground

*   Cedar Creek Golf Course (Located in Cedar Creek Area)

      David Boren Hiking Trail (**Page 42**)

      Overnight Trail Camping (**Page 51**)

      Indian Nation Dual-Use Trail—Hiking And Biking (**Page 48**)

*   Forest Heritage Center (**Page 38**)

      Nature Trails (**Page 40**)

  9   Tennis

      Trout Fishing (**Page 53**)

Things To Do In The Park

Broken Bow Reservoir

259 A North

Hwy 259

Lower Mt Fork

Forest Heritage Center & Gift Shop ④

259 A South

Broken Bow

Beavers Bend Area

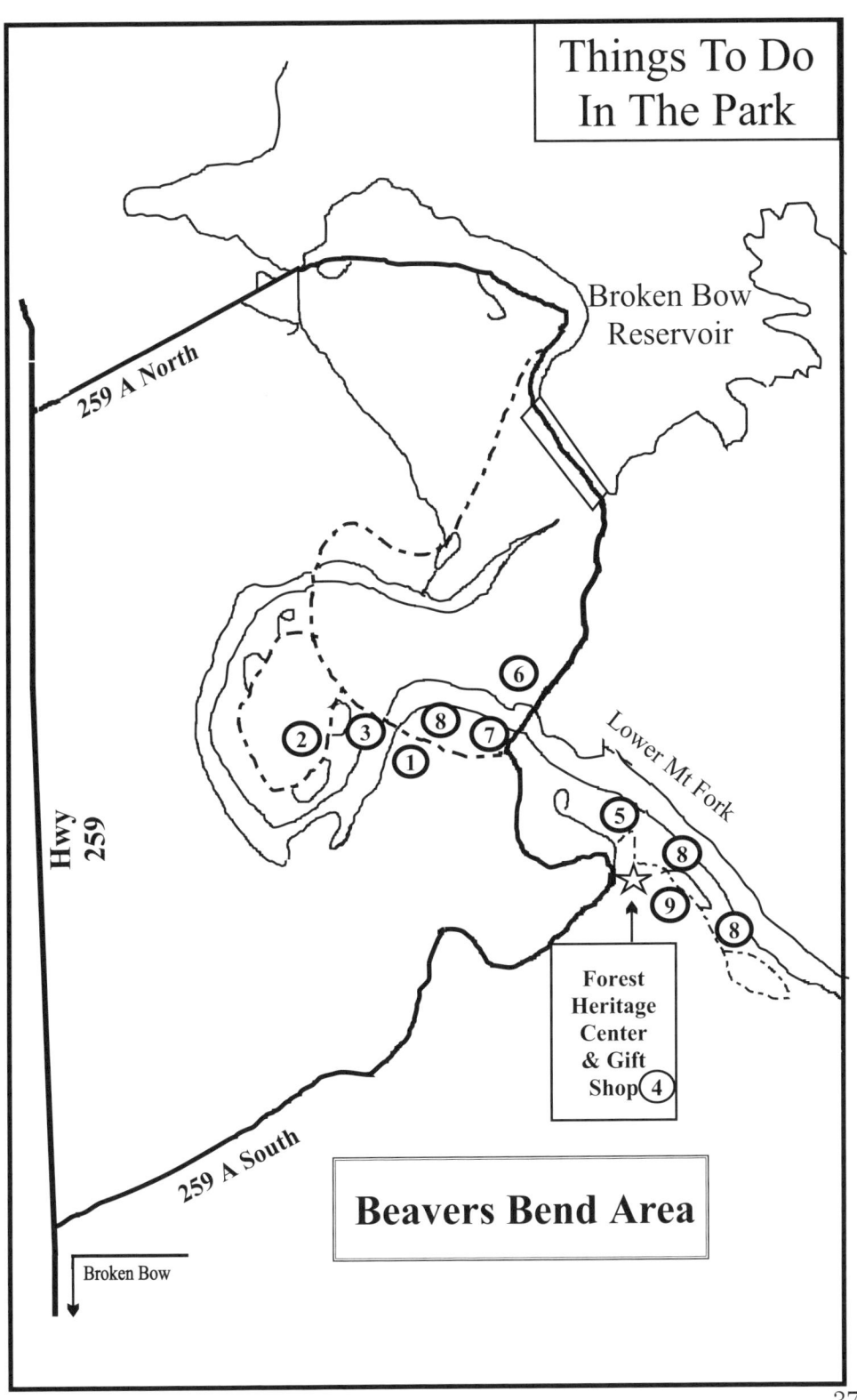

The Forest Heritage Center And Museum (580) 494-6497 is a **MUST** place to visit! It is the first building on your right after you enter the park on Hwy 259A. This **free** museum also houses the Park information center, cabin reservation center and gift shop.

The center was founded in 1975 for the purpose of 1) informing and educating the public about forestry in the South; 2) demonstrating proper natural resource management; and 3) creating a forestry museum to explain the past and explore the future.

The centerpiece of the museum's educational exhibits are the 14 murals painted by Smokey Bar artist, Harry Rossoll. These dioramas or murals tell the story of forestry and how it has impacted our lives throughout history. The museum also includes a fabulous historic photograph collection, chainsaw collection and wood art gallery. In 1996 a wood art gallery was established to showcase some of the finest works of art utilizing wood as a medium that could be shown.

Also part of the Forest Heritage Center and Museum is a 1.1 mile loop nature trail with markers to help you identify 57 different trees, plants, and shrubs native to the area. The center offers a "Tree Trail" guide book for a nominal charge to help you identify and learn more about the native vegetation.

Beavers Bend Fly Shop
Sid Ingram (580) 494-6071 Shop
(580) 642-6771 Home

Beavers Bend Fly Shop is located next to the Beavers Bend Area inside the Beavers Bend State Park And Resort. Besides offering a full service tackle shop that can provide all your tackle needs for that special fishing trip, the fly shop also offers fishing guide services and flycasting instruction for new fishermen. They can also provide you with important information such as fishing reports, maps, photos and more. The Mountain Fork River that flows past the fly shop is a state designated trout stream which is 12 miles long and holds thousands of rainbow trout and brown trout. The Oklahoma Fish And Game Department stocks nearly 4000 fish every other Thursday. Beavers Bend is a year-round fishery located only 3 hours from Dallas/Ft. Worth.

Beavers Bend Nature Center
(580) 494-6556

A year-round naturalist and a well-stocked nature center make possible a program lineup that includes campfire programs on the banks of the Mountain Fork River, nature hikes, arts and crafts classes, water sports, bingo, sunset hikes, nature films, and astronomy outings. The nature center offers many special "children oriented" programs on a daily basis so check their schedule when you first visit the park.

Beavers Bend Marina
(580) 494-6455
Located on Stevens Gap Road off Hwy 259N of Beavers Bend State Park And Resort
Water Skiing, Jet Boating, Fishing, Swimming
www.beaversbendmarina.com

Beavers Bend Lake is one of the clearest lakes in the country and is a great place to fish, swim, water ski or just explore the isolated shoreline that is part of the Quachita National Forest.

The Beavers Bend Marina offers boat, jet ski, and houseboat rentals as well as a store, gas, pump-outs and a full-time mechanic to take care of all your boating needs. They have one houseboat to rent that sleeps up to ten people. Rent it for several days and find your own secluded beach along the 180 miles of Broken Bow Lake shoreline to get away from it all. The marina also rents three person Yamaha's and Seadoo's by the hour or by the day and a wide selection of party barges for, well, that special party. The party barges are rented by the hour or by the day. If your interest is tube/ski rentals they have that too, and again you can rent by the hour. They also have a number of annual slip rents for all sizes of boats, even house boats. If you have other boating needs, give Beavers Bend Marina a call, they can probably take care of it.

Cedar Creek Golf Course
(580) 494-6456
Hours are 7 AM – until sunset, 8 AM - 5 PM off season

This 18 hole golf course was carved out of the pine-laden wilderness area located next to the McCurtain County Wilderness Area. Fairways cascade through stands of pine, oak, and hickory and past deer, fox, and wild turkey. Several holes offer a fine view of Broken Bow Lake and the occasional glimpse of bald eagles. Cedar Creek, given a 5 Star rating by Golf Digest, is known for its narrow fairways and wooden roughs. The par-72 course has a pro shop, resident pro, and cart and club rentals; it is located nine miles north of the town of Broken Bow on US-259, a large sign announces its entrance. The clubhouse lies at the end of the road, about 3 1/2 miles east of the Hwy 259N turn-off.

Nature Trails, Hiking Trails, Overnight Backpacking, and Mountain Biking Trails

The trail system in Beavers Bend State Park and the adjacent Stephens Gap and Carson Creek areas offers a variety of different levels of trails to park visitors.

Some general safety tips before attempting any of these trails are:

1) Stay on the trail! The trails are marked. If you don't see trail markers located on the trees in front of you—stop and retrace your route until you see the trail markers.

2) Carry plenty of water. You'll need more water if the weather is hot and humid.

3) Supervise young children at all times. It wouldn't be a bad idea if they carried a whistle to use in an emergency.

4) Carry a map of the trail with you. Maps of the David Boren Hiking Trail (DBHT) and nature trails are available at the Forest Heritage Center and Nature Center.

5) Allow 30 minutes to 1 hour for each mile of trail to be hiked.

6) Spray yourself for ticks and chiggers before beginning and depending on the season, carry some mosquito repellent.

Nature Trails

Nature trails are the shortest, and for the most part, easiest to navigate on fairly level terrain. If you want to take the whole family for a leisurely walk through a nature wonderland, check out these trails first before trying the hiking trails. Children five years and older should be able to negotiate these trails.

Forest Heritage Tree Trail

This trail is a 1.1-mile loop trail that begins and ends at the Forest Heritage Center. The trail goes downhill until it reaches Beaver Creek. It follows a portion of the creek bottom then loops around and brings you back to the Forest Heritage Center. A series of informational signs about trees, animals and local vegetation are located along the trail. To remain on this trail, follow the wooden signs. The Beaver Creek Hiking Trail also follows a portion of Beaver Creek and is marked with red on white tree blazes, so be careful you don't cross trails and start following the wrong one.

Pine Ridge Nature Trail
This trail is about ¾ mile long, fairly easy to walk and starts across from the tennis courts. You will see a large trail head sign marking the start of this trail. This trail is marked with red on white tree blazes. This is a looping trail ending at the same place you started. The trail winds up the ridge, through a pine/hardwood forest then down through a bottomland forest filled with American holly trees.

Dogwood Nature Trail
This trail is about 1 mile long and loops back to where you started. The trail head is located in the Grapevine campground. The trail first follows along the Mountain Fork River then turns inland and passes through a pine/hardwood forest. You'll have to park your vehicle in the parking area and then walk back to the start of the trail. This is one of the easier trails to walk. It's a little rocky in spots but has no steep inclines to walk.

Cedar Bluff Nature Trail
This trail is a 1-mile loop and should be walked CLOCKWISE. Park your vehicle in the Dogwood campground parking area, and then walk across the road (Hwy 259A) to the trail head sign. Caution: This is also the entrance to the David Boren Hiking Trail System! Make sure you don't get on the wrong trail. At the trail head sign, start on your left (What direction?) and at each junction, (following the blue on white tree blazes) turn right and you will come out where you started. At the top of the trail is a picturesque view overlooking the Mountain Fork River.

Beaver Lodge Trail
This is a 1-mile long trail that does not loop back. You can start at either end of the trail. One trail head begins just below the spillway while the other trail head is located just off of Hwy 259A. Parking lots are located at both ends of the trail. If you enter the trail head from the parking lot just off of Hwy 259A the trail is very easy to walk and is wide and flat because it's actually an access road that follows the spillway run-off creek. The last 1/4-mile turns into an unmarked trail that still follows the Spillway run-off creek. On this section of the trail you will find a walk bridge that crosses the creek and takes you to a parking lot area. If you don't take the walk bridge and continue on the trail it will bring you to another parking lot located below the spillway. This is where people park and fish the Spillway Creek for trout. If you want to continue on the Indian Nations Hiking Trail from the parking area located at the bottom of the spillway, walk 200 yards up the parking lot access road to Hwy 259A, turn right and walk 200 yards back toward the tip of the spillway. Before you get to the spillway, the Indian Nations Hiking Trail will be located to your left.

Hiking Trails

David Boren Hiking Trail

Most of the hiking trails in the park are part of the David Boren Hiking Trail System (DBHT) named in honor of former Governor and current O.U. President, David Boren. In 1977 Gov. Boren authorized the funding for building this hiking trail system. No mountain biking is allowed on any of these trails. Mountain bikes are allowed on the Indian Nation All-Purpose Trail System located in the Stephens Gap Area. The DBHT trail begins at the south end of Beavers Bend State Park near Acorn campground and extends for nine miles intersecting with the Beaver Lodge Trail. **Please note this trail does not loop back.** You'll have to arrange for someone to pick you up or drop you off or be prepared to walk back. This trail is well marked with red on white tree blazes and mile markers posted every mile along the trail. The David Boren Trail, with 4 major trail heads, allows hikers to select the trail length and level of difficulty for their fitness level. More experienced hikers could choose to hike the entire trail camping out along the way (campsites must be at least 100 feet off the trail).

The DBHT system is more demanding than the nature trails and the terrain is more challenging. Children under the age of ten might not find it enjoyable and parents might have to carry the younger children as they become tired. It's also highly recommended that you carry more water than you would if hiking one of the nature trails. There are a few spots you can find water on this trail but it needs to be either boiled or filtered before drinking.

Approximate trail lengths for the DBHT sections:

South Park	1 mile
Lookout Mountain	1.5 miles
*Beaver Creek	1 mile
Deer Crossing	2 miles
*Cedar Bluff	1 mile
Skyline	5 miles
*Beaver Lodge	1 mile

*Not part of the DBHT trail system

Note: The Skyline trail has several steep inclines and is recommended only for experienced hikers.

DBHT Trail Sections Descriptions

South Park Trail
The South Park trail is a step up in difficulty from the nature trails. If a child can handle the nature trails then this would be the section of the hiking trail they should try first. (This trail section ends where it intersects with the Lookout Mountain trail and the Beaver Creek trail. **Make sure you take the Beaver Creek trail back to the Nature Center.**)

South Park trail starts at the southern end of the park, near Acorn campground. To get there from the Forest Heritage Center, follow the park road past the Nature Center for 1 mile to the Acorn campground parking area. Cross the park road and walk down a gravel road for about 40 yards to the trail head sign. This is the beginning of both the DBHT and the South Park trail. This section is about 1 mile long and is the easiest section of the DBHT trail to hike. There are no steep climbs, just moderately rolling terrain. The South Park trail ends after you cross Beaver Creek. Beaver Creek is spring fed and water is available if you travel up stream about 20 or 30 yards. All water should be boiled or filtered before drinking. At the South Park trail junction you can continue straight on the Lookout Mountain section of the DBHT or turn right on the Beaver Creek section for 1 mile. This will take you to the park road across from the Nature Center.

Beaver Creek Trail
The Beaver Creek trail follows Beaver Creek crossing it in several places. If it has rained recently you will probably get your feet wet. Follow the red on white tree blazes to the park road. The Forest Heritage Tree Trail follows close to this trail so make sure you stay on the correct trail. A part of this trail was the original road into the park built by the Civilian Conservation Corps in the 1930's. You'll also pass the homestead site of John Beavers who originally owned this land before it became a state park.

Lookout Mountain Trail
At the South Park/Beaver Creek trail junction, continue up a moderately steep grade. This section is about 1½ miles long. About ¾ of a mile along the trail you'll come to a rock marker. From here you'll have a panoramic view of the park area. As you continue on the trail there will be several steep areas you'll have to traverse so you might want to rest and take in the view. The Lookout Mountain trail intersects a new trail that takes you back to the Forest Heritage Center (½ mile) and with the Deer Crossing trail.

New Trail to Forest Heritage Center
This trail was built as a safe scenic hike back to the Forest Heritage Center. **For Safety Reasons, Do Not Walk the Road Back To the Forest Heritage Center.**

Deer Crossing Trail
The trail head for Deer Crossing trail is along Hwy 259A. Park your car on the opposite side of the road then cross over to the trail head marker (watch for traffic). This section is a little over 2 miles in length. It follows the contours of several hills with only two climbs of moderate increase in elevation. You'll know you're getting close to the end of the trail when you start down a long steep downhill section. After reaching the bottom of the downhill portion of the trail you'll come to a large trail intersection sign. At the trail intersection you have a choice of turning left onto the Skyline trail or right to Hwy 259A where a trail head is located about 400 yards down the trail. This trail is part of the Cedar Bluff Nature Trail.

Skyline Trail
The Skyline trail is 5 miles in length. The easiest way to get on the trail is park your vehicle at the Dogwood campground parking area, cross over Hwy 259A to the trail head marker (watch for traffic). You'll start on the Cedar Bluff trail. The Cedar Bluff trail is a looped trail so you can start in either direction. The trail to the left has a gradual rise while the trail to the right is a very steep uphill climb. Both trails will get you to the Skyline trail, the left trail is just easier. After starting the Skyline trail you'll have several short, steep, uphill and downhill climbs on soft gravel and rock so take your time so you don't sprain an ankle. About 8/10 of a mile after mile marker 5 you'll pass through a "high line" clearing. 100 yards further down the trail you'll cross a stream bed. If it's rained recently and the weather is just right, you might want to see a secluded waterfall surrounded by moss and ferns by turning right off the trail and following the stream bed for about 40 yards. If you get to mile marker 6 and haven't found the stream bed, go back about 100 yards. Be careful not to destroy the fragile vegetation located in this area. About two miles down this trail you'll cross over Bee Creek and again, if it's been raining expect to get your feet wet. Bee Creek is spring fed so you'll find water there year around. All water should be boiled or filtered before drinking.

If you continue about 50 yards further down the trail and look to your right, there is a camping area located just on the other side of Bee Creek. Another 50 yards further down the trail is a swimming hole so, make sure you take something to swim in. It's ok to swim here, but remember, you swim at your own risk. There is poison ivy in the camping area and on this stretch of trail so keep you eyes open.

Poison Ivy
The leaves of poison ivy consist of three pointed leaflets; the middle leaflet has a much longer stalk than the two side ones. The leaflet edges can be smooth or toothed but are rarely lobed. The leaves vary greatly in size, 0.31" to 2.16" in length. The leaves are reddish when they emerge in the spring, turn green during the summer, and become various shades of yellow, orange or red in the autumn. If in doubt remember, " leaves of three, let them be …."

After following Bee Creek and crossing it several times you'll cross it one more time and start up the steepest part of the entire trail system. If you didn't rest and take a swim in the swimming hole, now's the time you wish you had.

After Bee Creek, there are no more sources of water so make sure you have all the water you need for the next 3 miles. As you hike the ridge look to your right. Off in the distance you'll see the Broken Bow Lake Dam. Far below you is the Mountain Fork River. Do Not Attempt to Climb Down To The River. Several people have been seriously injured trying and no one's made it yet. After the climb out of Bee Creek, the trail is fairly level until you get near the end. Here you'll have a long downhill hike. When you cross the newly constructed footbridge, you are at the trails end. This is where the Skyline Trail intersects with the Beaver Lodge trail. If you turn right, down the Beaver Lodge trail, it's about 300 yards to the trail head parking area. If you turn left, it's about ¾ mile to the trail head parking area located near the spillway.

Scenic Overlook • ■ Spillway

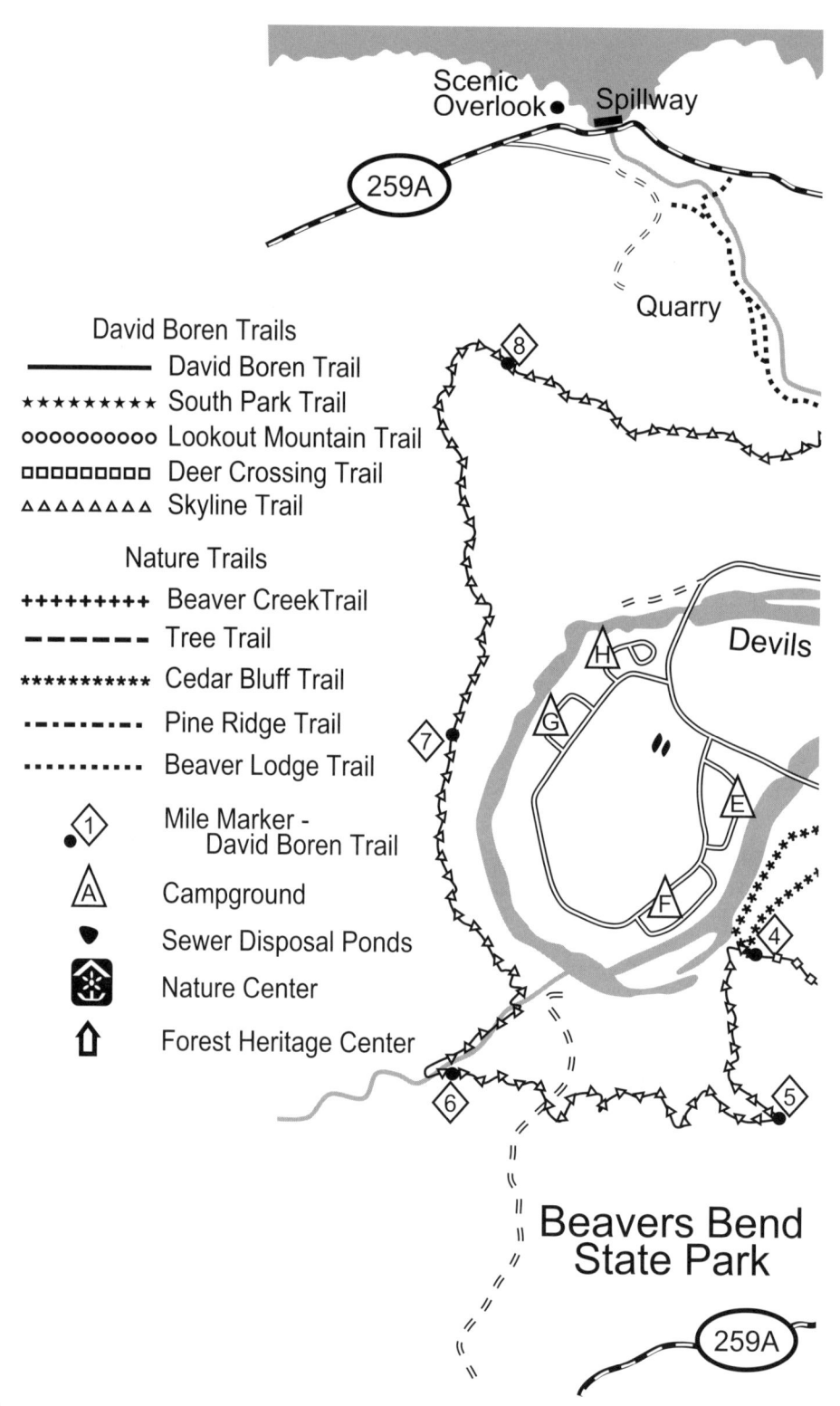

259A

Quarry

David Boren Trails
— David Boren Trail
✶✶✶✶✶✶✶✶✶ South Park Trail
ooooooooo Lookout Mountain Trail
▫▫▫▫▫▫▫▫▫ Deer Crossing Trail
△△△△△△△△ Skyline Trail

Nature Trails
+++++++++ Beaver Creek Trail
— — — — — Tree Trail
✶✶✶✶✶✶✶✶✶ Cedar Bluff Trail
— · — · — · Pine Ridge Trail
· · · · · · · · · Beaver Lodge Trail

◇1• Mile Marker - David Boren Trail
△A Campground
● Sewer Disposal Ponds
❄ Nature Center
⇧ Forest Heritage Center

Devils

Beavers Bend State Park

259A

46

47

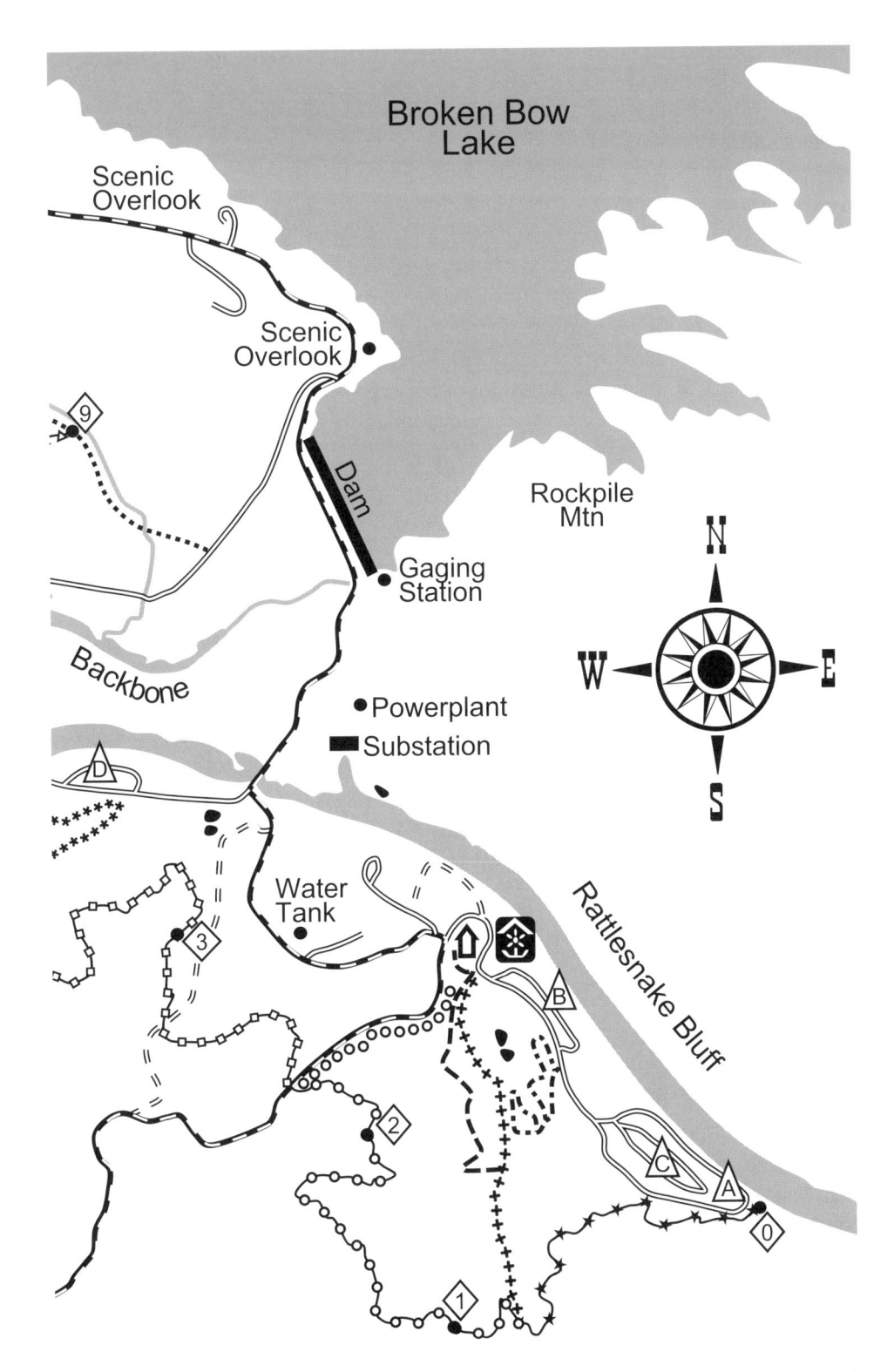

Indian Nation Dual-Use Trail System (Hiking and Biking)

Portions of this trail are near the park boundary so do not use this trail during the Deer Hunting Season (Gun). Check with the park office about the dates for Deer Hunting Season.

The Stephens Gap area is located next to Beavers Bend State Park and has about 6 miles of all-purpose trails that can be used for either hiking or mountain biking. This is the only trail system that mountain bikes are allowed on. The trails are not as well maintained or marked as the DBHT. Be observant of where you are on this trail system. If you don't see any red on white tree blazes marking the trail in front of you, stop and retrace your route until you see them. In some places the trail will follow an old overgrown access road then without warning veer off either left or right. Also unlike the DBHT, there are no mile markers on this trail system.

Indian Nation Trail Hwy 259A Spillway to Area 1 RV Camping Area Located just off the Lakeview Lodge Stephens Gap Area Road

The Indian Nation trail head is located just west of the Spillway on Hwy 259A. There's a parking area located there. This section of the trail is 4 miles long and not well marked so pay close attention to your surroundings at all times. The trail is mostly level with several short but moderately steep dips to numerous streambed crossings. You'll be at the halfway point of this trail when you cross a well-used gavel access road. The last several hundred yards of the trail is not marked at all. However if you look to your left across the ravine you'll see the Area 1 RV camping area of Stephens Gap located just off of the Lakeview Lodge Sevens Gap area road. Continue on the trail as it winds around and comes out near the restroom and parking area.

Indian Nation Trail Area 1 RV Camping Area Lakeview Lodge Sevens Gap Area Road to Carson Creek Area Road Trail Head

The trail head for this section of the Indian Nation trail is located across the road from the restrooms and parking area of Area 1 RV camping. Watch for traffic as you cross the road. This section of the trail is 2 miles long. The first part of the trail is marked with red on white tree blazes. At the halfway point of this trail you'll cross a high line access road. The trail will then take you down a steep ravine to a dry streambed. After you come out of the streambed, the trail is poorly marked. Some people have tied red streamers to the trees to help mark the trail. The trail ends at the trailhead on the Carson Creek area road.

Mountain Biking Trails

The Indian Nation trail in the Stephens Gap area is also an all-purpose trail that can be used for hiking or mountain biking. Bike this trail with caution! The trail is no wider than hiking trails, not clearly marked, and has tree limbs and other vegetation lying across the trail. There are also sharp downhill and uphill turns. I like to describe mountain biking this trail as, "If you like riding roller coasters but want more risk, and if your mountain bike is paid off and medical insurance is up to date, this might be the trail for you."

The park is planning to build another 4 to 6 miles of mountain biking trails in the Stephens Gap area over the next three years.

Indian Nation Dual-Use Trail

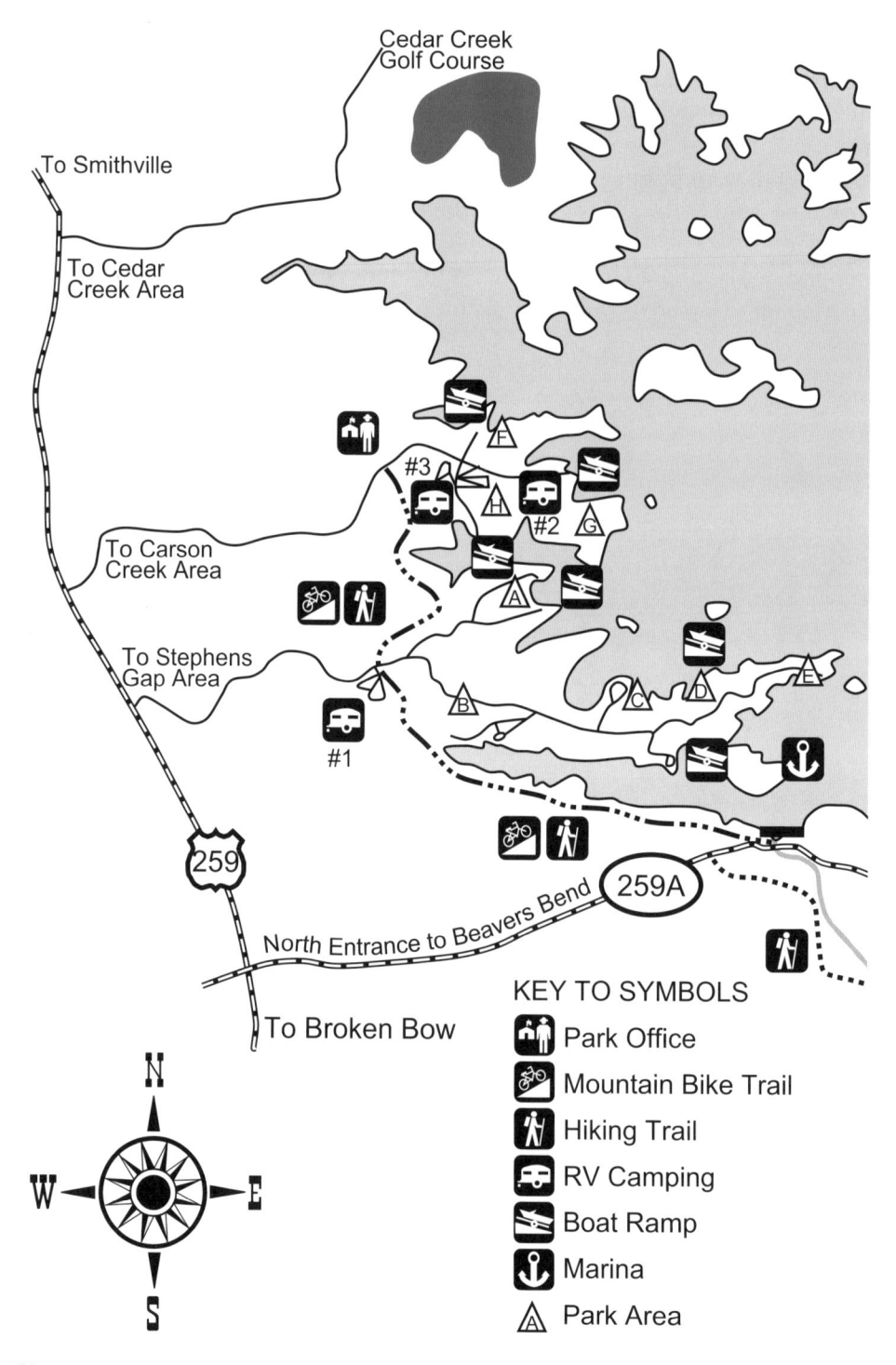

50

Overnight Trail Camping

Overnight trail camping is allowed on the DBHT. No permits are required. Your camp must be at least 100 feet off the trail and no open fires are permitted. From the beginning of the trail to mile marker 4, the terrain is really not suitable for setting up camp. Following are suggested areas that are level.

Mile Marker 4

When you reach mile marker 4 turn left, about 50 yards off the trail is a large cleared level area for overnight camping. If you go 20 yards further you'll see a section of the Skyline trail. For water and swimming turn right on the Skyline trail, go about 40 yards down the trail incline and look to your left for a path down to the Mountain Fork River. It's ok to swim here. Make sure you boil or filter the water before using.

Camping Between Mile Marker 5 and 6 (Skyline Trail)

There are about four or five good camping areas on this stretch of the trail. There is no water source so make sure you bring enough for drinking. You will also have to clear some rocks and vegetation. There are several camping spots after mile marker 5. 100 yards past on the left, 300 yards past, 800 yards past, ¾ of a mile past and 100 yards to your right, and just past the high line crossing to your left.

Bee Creek (Skyline Trail)

After hiking down a steep hill, you will cross Bee Creek to a large cleared camping area. 50 yards further down the trail and to your right on the other side of Bee Creek, is another camp area and 50 yards farther down the trail is a swimming hole. Be on the lookout for poison ivy in this area. After Bee Creek, there is no suitable area for camping.

Fishing

Anglers 10 years of age and older must have purchased and have in their possession a valid Oklahoma resident or nonresident fishing license. Also all anglers, regardless of age, must possess a special trout license for fishing. Both licenses may be purchased at the park reservation office located in the Forest Heritage Center.

Fishing License Information
Resident-
Fishing $20.00 a year
Fishing (2-day) $10.00
Youth Fishing (16 and 17 years old) $5.00 a year
Lifetime Fishing $200.00
Lifetime Fishing (60 and older) $30.00
Trout $10.00 a year
Youth Trout (17 years old and under) $5.00
Nonresident-
Fishing (Annual) $37.00
Fishing (5-day) $18.50
Lifetime Fishing $250.00
Trout $10.00 a year
Youth Trout (17 years old and under) $5.00
* *Also required for all fishing licenses this year is a FHL Fishing and Hunting Legacy permit for $5*

Broken Bow Lake
If fishing is your game this is the place to be. Broken Bow Lake, with over 180 miles of shoreline, is home to trophy largemouth bass, smallmouth bass, catfish and panfish. Broken Bow Lake is located eight miles north of Broken Bow on Hwy. 259 North, turn right on Lakeview Lodge Stephens Gap area road and follow it about three miles to its end.

Lower Mountain Fork River
The Lower Mountain Fork River flows through Beavers Bend Resort Park and is considered to be Oklahoma's premier trout location. Trout Fishing is allowed year around. Every other Thursday it is stocked with 4000 Rainbows and Browns. Many avid fishermen view this as the place to be since it holds the Oklahoma state record for the largest brown trout caught.

If you are a newcomer to the area, read carefully the Lower Mountain Fork River Trout Regulations listed below. Two places where you might try your luck, is just below the Spillway and Reregulation Dam; the locals know it as

(Rereg.). There is a parking area located just off of 259A below the Spillway. The quickest way to get to Rereg., located next to Mt. Fork Park, is from the Forest Heritage Center. Head west on 259A out of the park for about 2.1 miles. Just outside the park area turn left on a gravel road (the sign reads –A5 20 02.30) that winds around for about 5 miles and will then bring you to the road that leads to Rereg. Dam. Turn left and travel about 1.4 miles to Mt. Fork Park and the Rereg. Dam. This is also the area that most of the float trips begin. Note: If you turn right, the road will take you to Hwy 70.

Lower Mountain Fork River Trout Regulations

Trout Season: Year round.

Designated Trout Area/Size/Location: 12 mile portion of the Lower Mountain Fork River and its tributaries from Broken Bow dam downstream to U.S. Highway 70 bridge. About five miles of this designated trout stream lies within Beavers Bend State Park, which is six miles north of Broken Bow on U.S. Highway 259, in McCurtain County.

Bank Access/Boat Ramps: Access is unlimited within the state park. Below Beavers Bend State Park there are public access points at the Reregulation (Rereg.) Dam, Presbyterian Falls and the north side of the Hwy 70 E. bridge.

Special Regulations: Brown Trout Regulations (Entire Stream): Daily limit: one (1); Size limit: 20-inch minimum.

Zone I (Broken Bow spillway downstream to State Park Dam):
1. Rainbow trout - Daily limit: six (6); Size limit: none.
2. Use of bait and barbed hooks is permitted in Zone I.

Zone II (State Park Dam downstream to Reregulation Dam):
1. Use of bait or barbed hooks is prohibited in Zone II. Fishing is restricted to barbless hooks, artificial flies and lures only.
2. Possession of any trout less than 20-inches in size is prohibited.

Zone III (Reregulation Dam downstream to Hwy. 70 bridge):
Same as Zone I

NOTE: Total daily creel limit is six (6) rainbow trout, no more than one (1) may be 20 inches or longer from either Zones II or III, and one (1) brown trout 20 inches or longer.

Lower Mountain Fork Trout Area

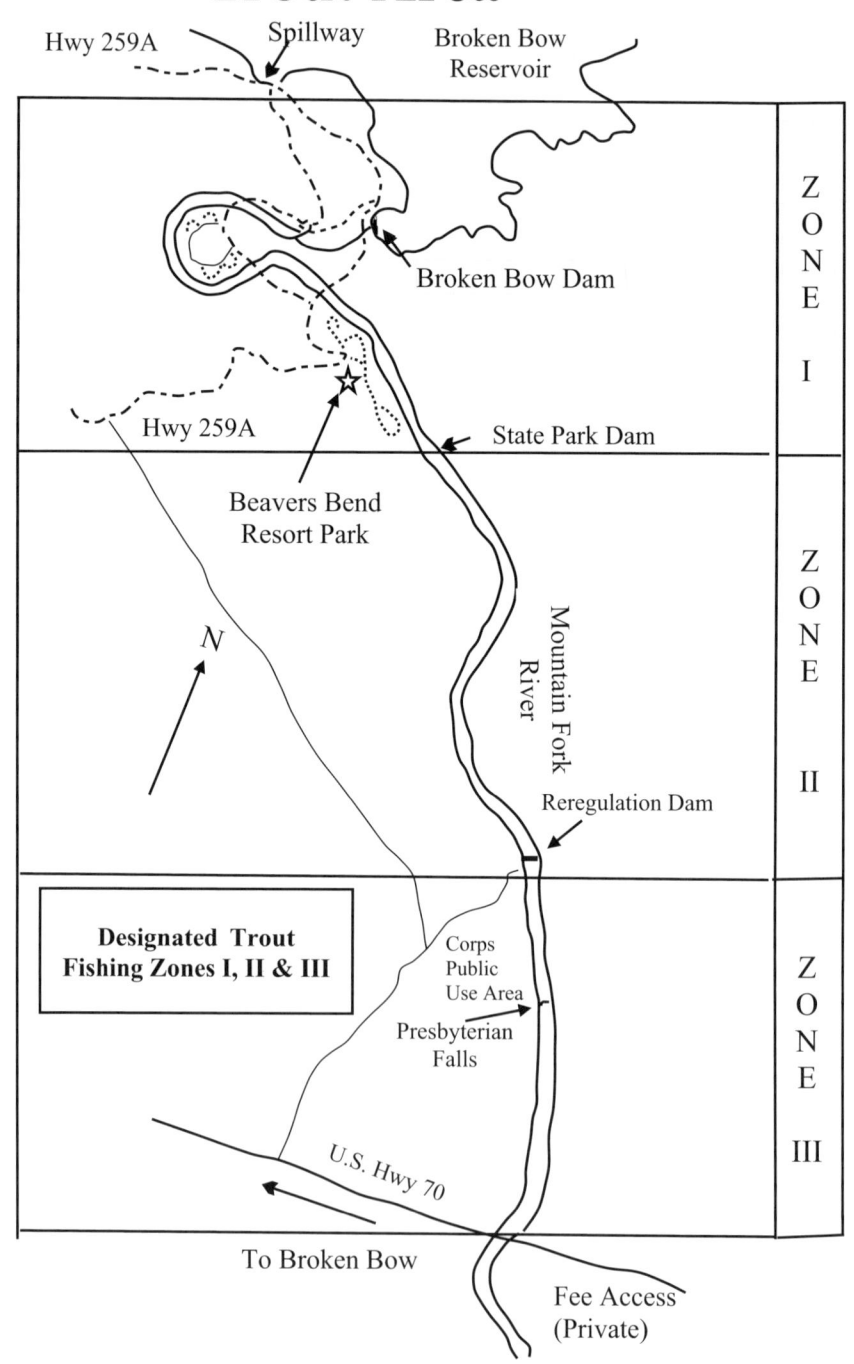

Hwy 259A — Spillway — Broken Bow Reservoir

Broken Bow Dam

Hwy 259A

State Park Dam

Beavers Bend Resort Park

N

Mountain Fork River

Reregulation Dam

Designated Trout Fishing Zones I, II & III

Corps Public Use Area

Presbyterian Falls

U.S. Hwy 70

To Broken Bow

Fee Access (Private)

ZONE I

ZONE II

ZONE III

54

Things To Do Outside The Park

Canoeing and Kayaking (**Page 56**)

Canoe Outfitters (**Page 60**)

Guided Hiking, Canoeing and Kayaking Trips (**Page 62**)

ATV/ORV Trail Riding/ Horseback Riding (**Page 64**)
Three Rivers WMA, Honobia Creek WMA
and Ouachita WMA Information and Regulations

Places to stay near ATV/ORV and HORSE TRAILS (**Page 71**)

Other Activities (**Page 72**)
    Fishing Guides
    Scuba Diving
    Trail Riding
    Hochatown Amusements
    McCurtain Cinema
    Rocket Roller Rink
    Stephens Gap Raceway

Museums (**Page 82**)

Canoeing and Kayaking the Mountain Fork River

Canoeing and kayaking the Mountain Fork River is a lot of fun but before you take your trip please read and follow these safety tips.

1. The first four miles, from the put-in to Hwy 70 east bridge **is not for small children,** many people spill their canoes in the rocky first five miles. The second part of the trip which is five miles from Hwy 70 east bridge to the take-out is much safer for young children. But as always, you as the parent must use your best judgment.
2. Always wear your safety vest, never take it off.
3. Make sure you wear a hat, have cover clothing for longer trips and carry sunblock even in cloudy weather.
4. Do not wear flip-flops!, They will not stay on if you tip your canoe. Buy a cheap pair of laced sneakers from a budget store. It will be the best investment you'll ever make.
5. Take plenty of water and if you take an ice chest make sure it latches so when you tip nothing falls out.
6. Take a towel to cover your neck or legs to prevent sunburn.

Lower Part of the Mountain Fork Below Broken Bow Lake

This is a must activity when visiting Beavers Bend Resort Park. There are several options to choose from. If all you want to do is canoe or kayak on a gentle stretch of the Mountain Fork River within the park you will find this opportunity just a short distance from all of the park campgrounds. For those who want more excitement, you need to check out canoeing and kayaking the Lower Mountain Fork River located south of the park just outside the park boundaries. The canoe and kayak outfitters are located several miles east of Broken Bow on Hwy 70. They will transport you to the put-in area and pick you up at the pull-out area, then transport you back to your vehicle. From the park it might take 15 to 20 minutes driving time to get to one of the outfitters, but it's well worth the drive.

Many believe the Lower Mountain Fork River is the most scenic river in Oklahoma. Here you will be canoeing and kayaking among miles of Cypress trees that are native only to this area of the state. The choices of trips offered by area outfitters are a 4 mile trip, 2 x 4 trip, 5 mile trip, 9 mile trip, and the 18 mile trip for overnight campers.

4-Mile Trip

The put-in for this trip is a public access park called Mt. Fork Camp Area (the locals call it Rereg.) located just below the Reregulation Dam. The trip ends four miles down river at the Hwy 70 bridge and will take about 2 ½ hours. The first four miles are very tricky and depending on whether or not the Corps of Engineers is releasing water from the dam upstream, (your outfitter will advise you of the current conditions) could be considered dangerous for small children. In this section of the river there are many rock gardens you have to maneuver around, several swift chutes to navigate through, and finally Presbyterian Falls that you have to find the best way over. Kayaks are better suited for this part of the river. If you have never kayaked before, don't worry, just get in and practice in the smooth water at the put- in point. After you get the feel for how to maneuver your kayak, watch how others are navigating through the rocks then make your choice of where to go. That's half the fun.

More people canoe than kayak so when given a choice, choose the canoe. You will see more people having problems maneuvering canoes in this section and having less fun than the kayakers. So, you make your own choice.

2 x 4 Trip

For those that want plenty of action and excitement this is a great trip consisting of doing the above four mile trip twice. Your outfitter will pick you up at the Hwy 70 bridge and shuttle you back to the start for one more run. When finished they will then shuttle you back to your vehicle. Estimated time for this trip is 5 hours.

5-Mile Trip

This portion of the trip begins at the Hwy 70 bridge, the same place the four mile trip ends. Compared to the first four miles this section of the river is gentle, relaxing and also quite scenic. You know you are nearing the end of the trip when you pass a number of beautiful houses with impressive decks overlooking the river on your right. This section of the river is suitable for young children. Remember life vests should be worn at all times. It's more comfortable to canoe this section than kayak it, if you did the first section in a kayak check with your outfitter about switching to canoes if you are doing both sections. It also would not be a bad idea to take a small ice chest with you on this section. Estimated time for this trip is 2 1/2 hours.

9-Mile Trip

This trip is a combination of the 4 mile and 5 mile trips. It's an all day trip so make sure to bring an ice chest along. As I have already mentioned, check with your outfitter about switching from kayaks to canoes after you complete the first four miles. Estimated time for this trip is 5 hours.

18-Mile Trip

If you enjoy combining camping out under the stars with canoeing this just might be your trip. One the first day you complete the nine mile trip mentioned above, spend the night sleeping on the banks of the Mountain Fork River and then the next day complete the last nine miles. You will need to provide your own camping equipment for this trip. The outfitter will see that it is delivered to you overnight camping spot.

Upper Part of the Mountain Fork River above Broken Bow Lake

This section of the Mountain Fork River is only canoed or Kayaked in the spring when the water level is high. While the Lower Mountain Fork River water level is regulated by the Army Corps of Engineers thus is predictable, the Upper Mountain Fork River is not and the water level is dependent on spring rains. This section is **not recommended** for first-timers or people with beginners level experience. Contact the same canoe and kayak outfitters that operate the Southern Mountain Fork River.

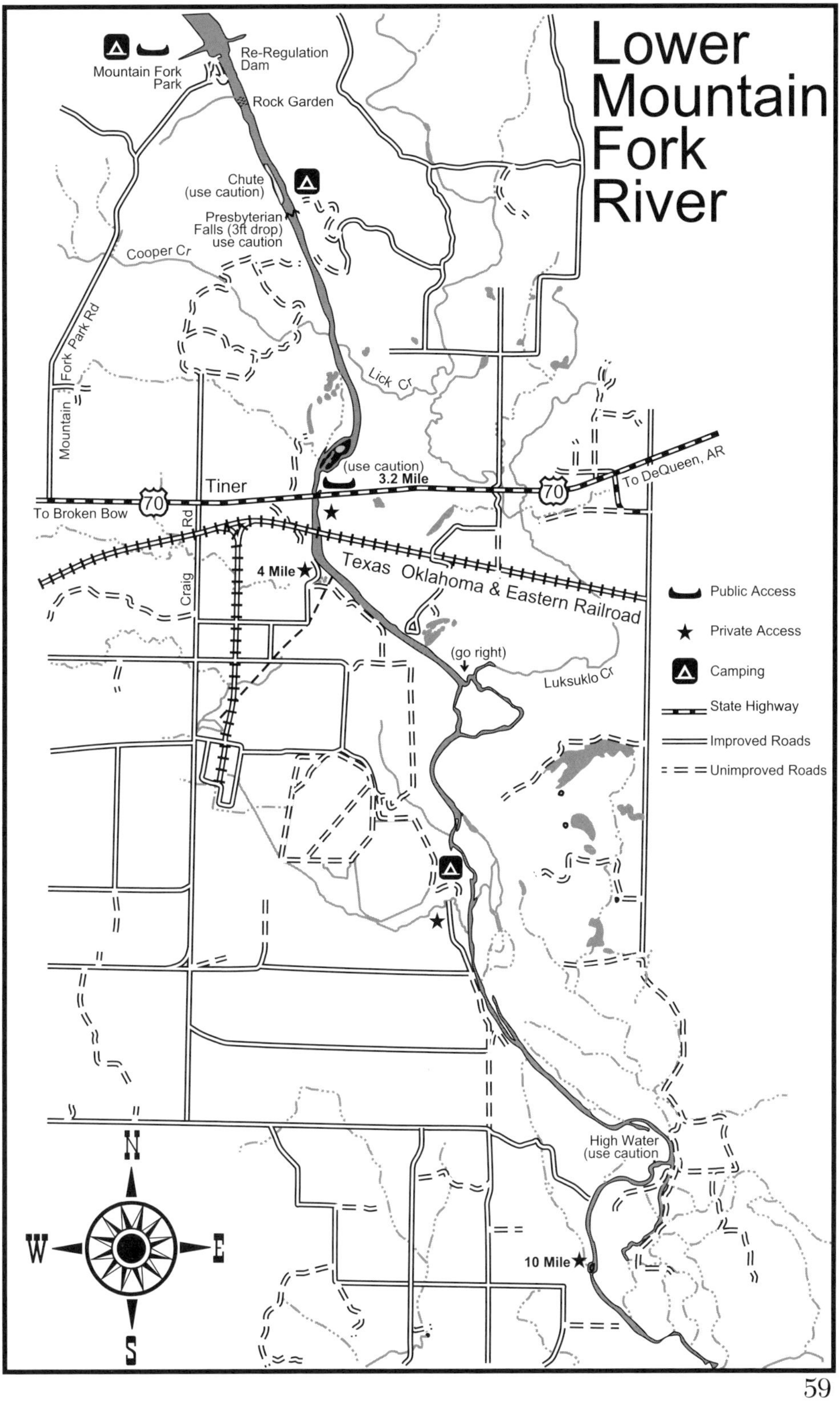
Lower Mountain Fork River
Mountain Fork Park
Re-Regulation Dam
Rock Garden
Chute (use caution)
Presbyterian Falls (3ft drop) use caution
Cooper Cr
Mountain Fork Park Rd
Lick Cr
(use caution)
3.2 Mile
Tiner
70
To Broken Bow
Craig Rd
To DeQueen, AR
4 Mile
Texas Oklahoma & Eastern Railroad
(go right)
Luksuklo Cr
Public Access
Private Access
Camping
State Highway
Improved Roads
Unimproved Roads
High Water (use caution)
10 Mile
N
W
E
S

Canoe Outfitters

1. **Ambush Adventures**
   Broken Bow, OK

2. **AKA Canoe Rental**
   Broken Bow, OK

3. **Ace Canoe and Kayak Rental**
   Broken Bow, OK

*4. **Beavers Bend White Water Canoe and Kayak Rentals**
   (Lower and Upper Mt. Fork River)
   (580) 584-6594
   Hwy 70 East, Broken Bow
   www.beaverbendwhitewater.com

Located just 3.5 miles east of Broken Bow, Beavers Bend White Water Canoe and Kayak Rentals is easy to locate and centrally located for quick access to the popular Mountain Fork River's put-in and pull-out points. Their friendly staff will be waiting for you when you finish your water adventure.

*5. **WW Trading Post and Canoe Sales and Rentals**
   Broken Bow, OK
   (Lower Mt. Fork River)
   (580) 584-6856
   www.wwcanoes.com

Whether it is for a half day or overnight, WW Trading Post and Canoe Rentals has an exciting trip for you. For your safety, the minimum age requirement is 6 years-old with adult supervision.
They are located 5 miles east of Broken Bow on Hwy 70. Then turn north at their WW Trading Post sign on the Mountain Fork Park road. Then travel 1 mile and you'll find them on the left side of the road.

6. **Wild Goose Canoe and Kayak Rentals**
   Broken Bow, OK

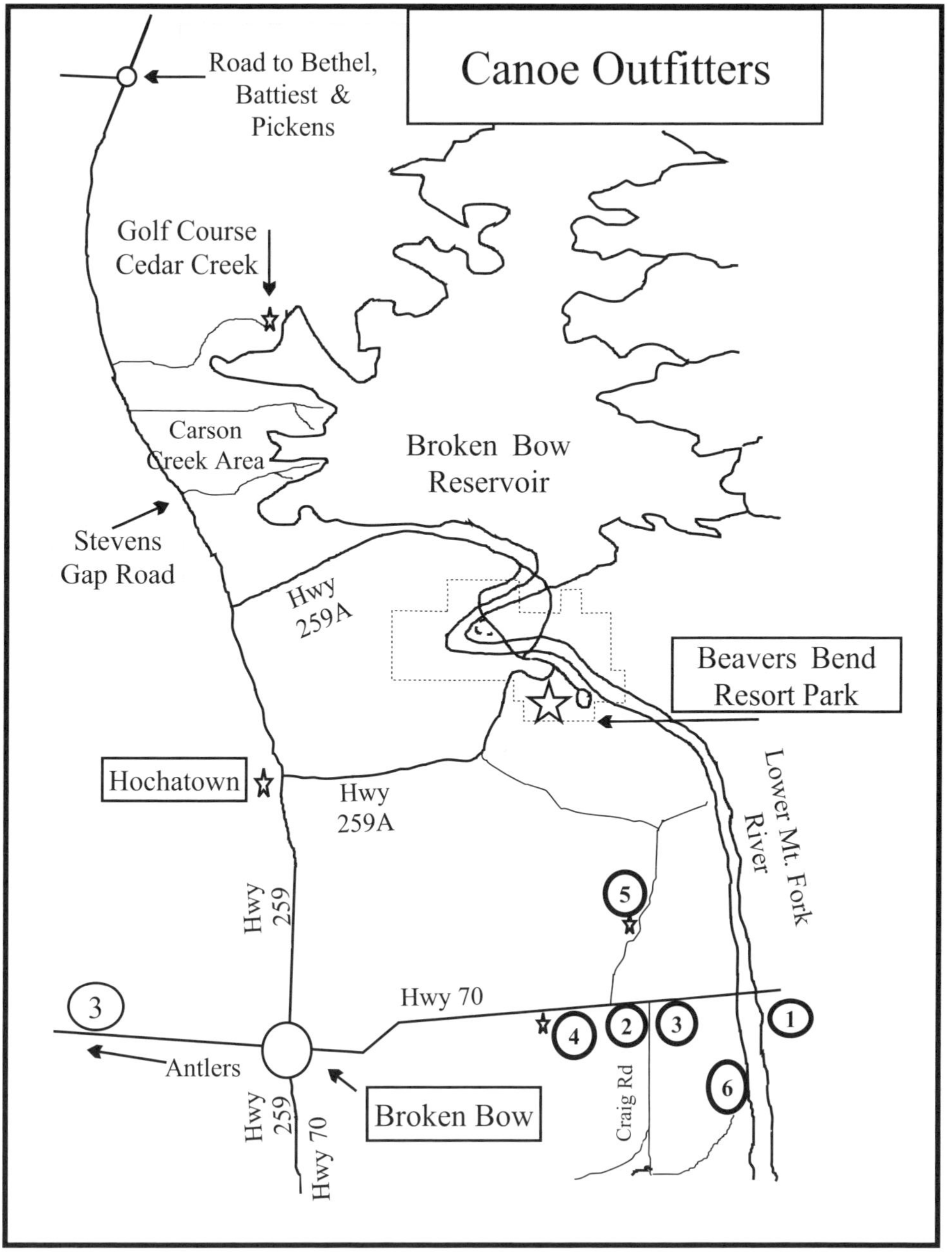
Canoe Outfitters
Road to Bethel, Battiest & Pickens
Golf Course Cedar Creek
Carson Creek Area
Broken Bow Reservoir
Stevens Gap Road
Hwy 259A
Beavers Bend Resort Park
Hochatown
Hwy 259A
Lower Mt. Fork River
Hwy 259
5
Hwy 70
3
4
2
3
1
Antlers
6
Craig Rd
Hwy 259
Hwy 70
Broken Bow

<u>Guided</u> Hiking, Canoeing and Kayaking Trips

Outback Guides
1(918) 446-5956

Outback Guides has over thirty years of experience guiding wilderness trips for many different diverse groups: youth, professional, private clients, senior citizens and Boy Scout and Girl Scout troops. For those interested in a more in-depth experience when visiting Beavers Bend Resort, Outback Guides offer you a choice of two outdoor adventures. The hiking and overnight camping will be done in the Park on the David Boren Hiking Trail and the canoeing and kayaking will be on the Lower Mountain Fork.

Wilderness Adventure Sampler One
4 Day Backpacking, Kayaking and Canoeing

Learn the basics of backpacking, backpacking equipment, kayaking and canoeing.
4 days/3 nights sleeping under the stars (minimum 8 people).

This trip is ideal for those that want to know more about backpacking. This is an educational trip on how to have a safe and fun backpacking experience. On this trip we will cover everything from A-Z that you need to know about backpacking and backpacking equipment. Some of the areas covered are:

How to plan a trip.
What's the best way to get a camping permit?
How to get the best equipment at an affordable price.
What to look for when buying a sleeping bag, tent, backpack and cook stove.
How to plan and prepare a meal .
Safety considerations.

We will be camping at primitive backcountry campsites in Beavers Bend Resort Park one of Oklahoma's most scenic parks located in the Kiamichi Mountains of Southeastern Oklahoma. This trip is for those that want to know more about backpacking. We have also included both kayaking and canoeing on this trip.

We will spend the first two days backpacking; learning how to pack and adjust your backpack, find good camping sites, set up tents, cook in the outdoors over light-compact stoves and filter water for drinking. The next two days we will both kayak and canoe 18 miles of the scenic Mountain Fork River. You will first learn to kayak then test your abilities as we kayak a very challenging part of the Mountain Fork River. We will then switch to canoes for the rest of the trip, spending one more night camping on the rivers edge.

Trip package includes:

1. Experienced guides.
2. All fees including cost of kayak and canoe.
3. All food needed and camping gear. (Sleeping bag, tents, backpack, and cook stove)

Call For Price.

Wilderness Adventure Sampler Two
2 Day Backpacking, Kayaking and Canoeing

For those whose time is more limited we also have a Two Day Wilderness Adventure Sampler. This includes one day backpacking with overnight wilderness camping and one full day of kayaking and canoeing. We will cover the basics of backpacking but because of the limited time, not to the depths as the 4 day trip.

Call For Price.

(If you are interested in a seminar on identifying edible plants and the medicinal properties of wild plants and flowers, call us.)

Call Outback Guides at (918) 446-5956 for reservations
(Group size 5 – 9)

To check out our trips and dates on line go to: **www.outbackguides.com**

ATV and ORV Riding and Use of Horses

ATV and ORV riding and use of horses are not permitted in Beavers Bend Resort Park. However they are allowed on state and public land adjacent to or within close proximity to the Park. The three state and public land areas nearby are the Three Rivers Wildlife Management Area (WMA) and Honobia (Hoe-na-bee) Creek Wildlife Management Area (WMA) and the Ouachita (Wash-it-ta) National Forest. People planning to enter these areas need to be aware that regulations, permits and fees may be different in each of these areas.

Three Rivers Wildlife Management Area (WMA) and the Honobia Creek Wildlife Management Area

Three Rivers Wildlife Management Area (WMA) and the Honobia Creek Wildlife Management Area Telephone Number: 1 (580) 242-5720

Three Rivers Wildlife Management Area

The Three Rivers Wildlife Management Area (WMA) created in 1998 encompasses approximately 450,000 acres of public recreation land for public use. It was formed through a cooperative agreement between the Oklahoma Department of Wildlife Conservation and the Landowner, Weyerhaeuser Company. The Three Rivers WMA also meshes with public lands of the Ouachita National Forest. Regulations, permits and fees are different in each of these areas.

Camping and Facilities

No designated camping areas exist, but primitive camping is allowed everywhere on the WMA. Campfires are allowed but during dry periods call the local WMA office 1 (580) 242-5720 for current information about any possible "fire ban".

Trail head and Parking

There are no official trail heads or parking areas in WMA. Some people will find an area along the dirt or gravel roads to pull off and park—be aware these areas are not secure. Others will off load their equipment and park their vehicles in a more secure area.

The following information was taken in whole or in part from various state publications. For more information including a free detailed map of the Three Rivers WMA and Honobia Creek WMA which also includes the Ouachita National Forest area surrounding Beavers Bend call the Department of Wildlife at 1 (405) 521 2739. Information is also provided at the web site www.wildlifedepartment.com

The "Land Access Fee" is required of all persons who hunt, fish or otherwise use the Three Rivers WMA. Only legal residents of Oklahoma who are under 18 years of age on the first day of the current calendar year or who are 64 years of age or older are exempt from the permit requirements. A $5, three-day special use land access permit is available to residents for nonhunting or nonfishing related activities, unless in possession of the $16 annual access permit.

By definition, this is a land ACCESS permit. So whether camping, horseback riding, hiking, sightseeing, birdwatching, or any other activity, you must possess the land access permit or have proof of exemption. The purpose is that all users equally share in maintaining the area. As an added bonus, the permit also allows access to the nearby Honobia Creek WMA.

Acquire your permit at any Oklahoma hunting and fishing license vendor throughout the state. All Oklahoma annual licenses and permits are filled out on a Universal License Form. The license vendor simply fills in a special code for each individual license or permit you purchase at a time. For example, if you choose to purchase an annual hunting and fishing combination license and a Land Access Fee (Permit) on the same day, you will receive only one universal license form coded for each item. However, if you purchase these individually on different days, you will receive a separate universal license form for each. This Land Access Fee (Permit) is NOT included with a lifetime hunting or fishing or combination license.

Since the Wildlife Department does not own this land, the land access fee is the only way to pay for the cost of law enforcement and management on the Three Rivers WMA. Funds generated through the sale of access fees will be used exclusively to manage this area.

By faithfully purchasing the land access permit annually, you become a vital steward or stakeholder to this land, with a vested interest in improving its potential. Think of it as your own personal lease with wildlife managers improving it daily just for you – and all for just $16/$25 a year.

Land Access Fee
Land Access Fee (Permit) may be purchased several ways.

- Permits are available at any Oklahoma hunting and fishing license vendor.
- Permits can also be purchased over the phone using your credit card by calling 1 (800) 223-3333.
- All licenses and permits offered by the Department may also be purchased through the Department's web site
www.wildlifedepartment.com

Per Person Land Access Fee (Permit)

$16 Resident
$25 Nonresident
$5 Resident 3-Day*
* For nonhunting and nonfishing activities * Only for Oklahoma Residents

General Regulations Governing Use of Three Rivers WMA For ORV/ATV and Horse Use

1. Permit Requirements:
   All persons who hunt, fish or otherwise use the Three Rivers WMA or the Honobia Creek WMA must possess a valid annual Land Access Permit or proof of exemption.

2. License Requirements:
   All persons carrying a firearm, bow and arrow, or anyone fishing on Three Rivers WMA must possess a valid hunting, fishing or combination license unless exempt.

3. Group Activities:
   Any activity involving groups of 25 individuals or more must receive prior written approval from the area biologist.

4. Camping:
   Camping is limited to a maximum of fourteen (14) days.

5. Building and Private Development:
   No permanent or temporary structures (buildings, earthworks, boat docks, etc.) may be constructed on Three Rivers WMA.

6. Vehicles:
   A. Except as otherwise noted, all motorized vehicles are required to stay on the roads designed as open for public or hunter use. There are no exceptions for motorcycles, four-wheel drive vehicles, snowmobiles or all-terrain vehicles.
   B. Off-road vehicles (ORV) and all-terrain vehicles (ATV) may be ridden on roads owned and maintained by the Weyerhaeuser Company and managed by the Oklahoma Department of Wildlife Conservation as part of Three Rivers WMA. ORV/ATV use on county roads or state highways must comply with (state law) Title 47 regulations.
   C. Maximum speed on Three Rivers WMA roads shall be 25 mph.

D. Travel on roads which are gated and locked, blocked by earthen mound, or otherwise designated as closed is prohibited, unless otherwise specified in the annual regulations for non-ambulatory persons holding valid permits accessing designated non-ambulatory access areas.

E through H deal with hunting restrictions.

7. Littering:
Disposal of garbage, trash, refuse, litter, sewage, debris or any other form of solid waste is prohibited.

8. Use of Horses:
Horses and mules may be used anytime on established roads and trails open for public use unless otherwise posted. During deer primitive and deer gun seasons, riders must wear both a head covering and an outer garment above the waistline consisting of daylight fluorescent orange totaling not less than 400 square inches.

9. Theft or Vandalism:
   A. It is unlawful for any person to shoot at, deface, damage, destroy, remove or steal all or part of physical structures, any equipment or machinery, fences, or fencing materials, cattle guards, gates, signs or any other state-owned property on Department-managed lands.
   B. It is unlawful to cut, dig, damage or remove crops, trees, shrubs, timber (including dead standing trees) water, gravel, sand, earth, rocks, materials or other natural resources other than legally harvested fish and wildlife from Three Rivers WMA without prior written approval from the Wildlife Department.

Honobia Creek Wildlife Management Area

The Honobia (Hoe-na-bee) Creek WMA is located in the heart of the Ouachita Mountains of Southeastern Oklahoma. This vast area includes over 130,000 acres of land and 37 miles of streams for outdoor enthusiasts to explore. Honobia Creek is owned by two different private investment groups – John Hancock Mutual Life Insurance Co. and Renewable Resource, LLC. Through cooperative agreements, the Wildlife Department manages the wildlife while helping to discourage unlawful activities, while in return the two landowners have agreed to keep these lands open to the public. Regulations, permits and fees are the same as the Three Rivers WMA and are listed above.

For more information including a free detailed map of the Three Rivers WMA and the Honobia Creek WMA call the Department of Wildlife at 1 (405) 521 2739. Information is also provided at the web site www.wildlifedepartment.com

All-Terrain Vehicles (ATV) and Off-Road Vehicles (ORV) Riding

Nobody likes regulations, but if irresponsible ATV and ORV use continues to cause unacceptable impacts to the wildlife management area, then strict regulations and enforcement and/or limited, seasonal ATV use will become necessary to ensure the protection of this privately owned, publicly accessible land.

OFF-ROAD USE IS STRICLY PROHIBITED:

- All motorized vehicles, including but not limited to ATVs, must remain on maintained logging roads unless otherwise posted.
- Driving over or around earthen mounds, gates, or signs is prohibited.
- Driving on powerline, seismic line, pipeline, and railroad right-of-ways is prohibited.
- Driving in streambeds and adjacent to creeks is prohibited unless following an existing, maintained logging road.
- ATV/ORV use on county roads or state highways must comply with State Law Title 47 regulations.

(Please refer to General Regulation 36 for additional vehicle use restrictions.)

Those ATV and ORV riders not adhering to the above regulations cause serious detrimental impact to the wildlife management area. Specifically, riding off-road quickly destroys the vegetation on the forest floor that is important to wildlife for nesting, loafing, and escape cover, as well as food. Without adequate vegetation on the forest floor, soil erosion becomes a serious problem. The direct disturbance of the vehicle not only degrades the quality but also the availability of the habitat for use by wildlife. As the off-road disturbance continues, deer, turkey, quail, furbearers, etc. will choose to move to habitats with less disturbance. Please do your part by remaining on maintained logging roads and informing other ATV/ORV riders of the importance of following all regulations.

Ouachita Wildlife Management Area
McCurtain Unit
Ouachita (Wash-it-ta) National Forest (McCurtain Unit)
Telephone Number: 1 (580) 286-6564

The Ouachita National Forest covers 1.8 million acres in central Arkansas and southeastern Oklahoma. The forest is managed for multiple uses, including timber and wood production, watershed protection and improvement, habitat for wildlife and fish species (including threatened and endangered ones), wilderness area management, minerals leasing, and outdoor recreation. Ouachita WMA— McCurtain Unit covers 111,000 acres in central and southern McCurtain County in the southeast corner of the state. The Broken Bow Subunit is located north of Broken Bow, surrounding Broken Bow Lake and the Glover River.

Loblolly pine plantations and upland hardwood forests dominate the 111,000 acres found within the Broken Bow Unit. This area contains the Ouachita mountain foothills and also surrounds the Lower Mountain Fork River. This portion of the WMA was acquired as part of a Forest Service/Weyerhaeuser land exchange in 1997.

For more information including a free detailed map of the Ouachita National Forest area surrounding Beavers Bend which also includes the Three Rivers WMA and Honobia Creek WMA call the Department of Wildlife at 1 (405) 521 2739.

Camping and Facilities:
There are no designated camping facilities in this area of the Ouachita National Forest, however primitive camping is permitted. Campfires are allowed but during dry periods call the local Ouachita National Forest office 1 (580) 286-6564 for current information about any possible "fire ban".

No fees or permits are required when using this area of the Ouachita National Forest. Permits are required when using the Three Rivers WMA which is adjacent to Ouachita National Forest; users need to be aware which area they are in at all times. Riding in closed areas and off of the open unpaved roads may result in fines up to $300.

Regulations for use of ORV, ATV and horses are the same as those for the Three Rivers WMA.

Trail head and Parking
There are no official trail heads or parking areas in this area of the Ouachita National Forest. However, many people park in an area located two miles north of the golf course.

McCurtain County Public Use Lands - Area Map

- Beavers Bend & Hochatown State Parks
- Ouachita National Forest
- McCurtain County Wilderness Area & Walk-in Turkey Areas
- Three Rivers Wildlife Management Area

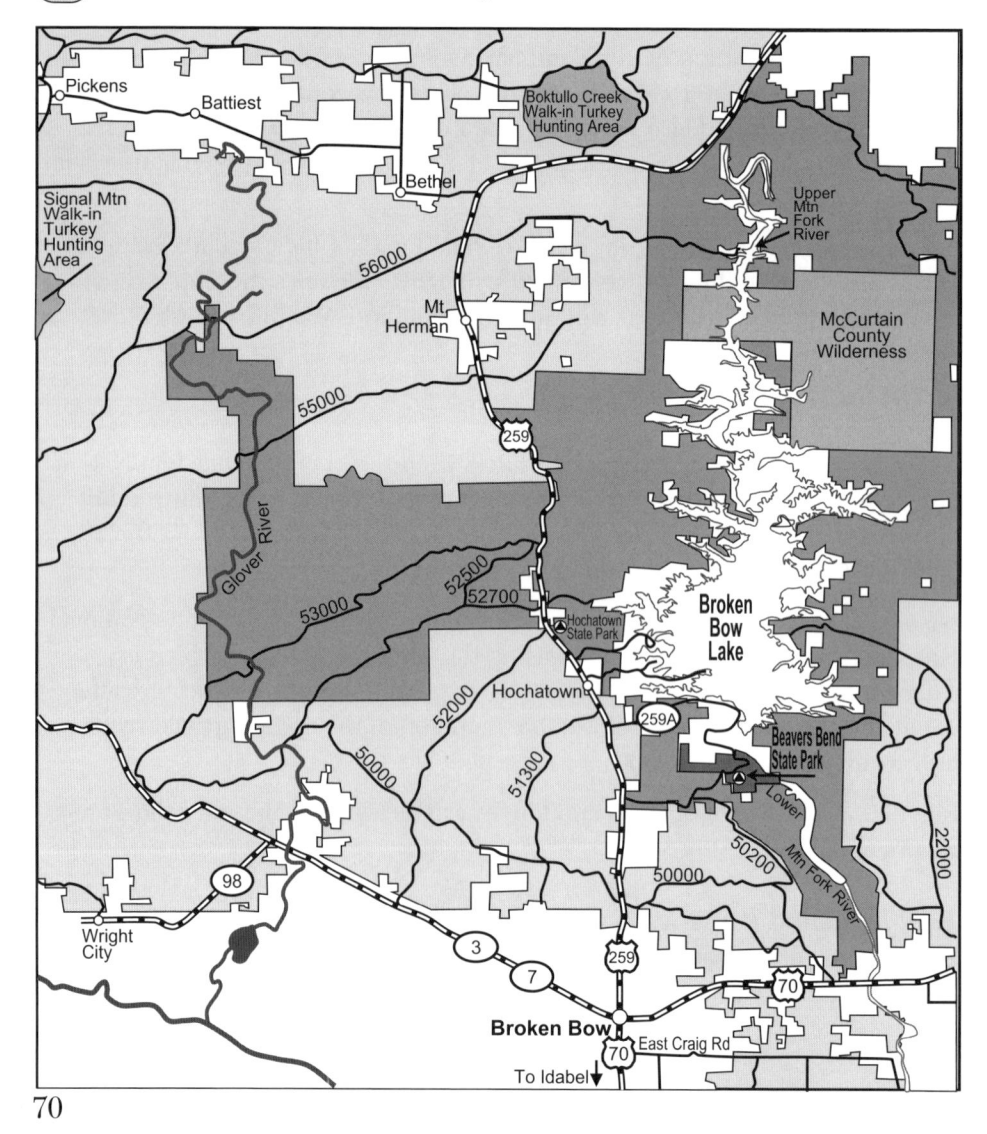

ATV Trail Riding/Horseback Riding

Horseback Riding:

A to Z Guest Ranch
North of Smithville
(580) 244-3729
atozguestranch.com

Bar 4 L Boarding Stables
Horseback Riding
(580) 212-2847

Crooked River Cabins
Horseback riding and ATV trails
3 miles N Hwy 259
(580) 241-5709
www.crookedrivercabins.com

Timberwolf Cabins
12 miles N Hwy 259
(580) 494-6363
www.timberwolfcabins.com

Tree Top View Cabins
Horseback riding and ATV trails
25 miles N Hwy 259
(580) 241-5599 or Fax (580) 241-5356
www.treetopviewcabins.com

Ponderosa Cabins
Horseback riding and ATV trails
Pickens, OK 74752
(580) 241- 5555 or 5453
www.ponderosacabinsok.com

Whip-Poor-Will Resort
ATV trails nearby
12 miles N Hwy 259
(580) 494-6476
www.okresort.com

Wilderness Lakefront Resort
ATV trails nearby
(580) 241-5304
www.lakefrontresort.com

Other Area Activities

Fishing Guides and Fishing Gear

*1 Three Rivers Fly Shop
Route 4, Box 27-1
Broken Bow, OK 74728
Located 6 miles north of Broken Bow on Hwy. 259
1 (580) 494-6115
www.threeriversflyshop.com

Owned and operated by Jesse and Linda King, Three Rivers Fly Shop is one of the largest fly fishing stores in Oklahoma and offers a host of top quality products to satisfy all your fly fishing needs. They are located on Highway 259 just across the street from the main entrance to Beavers Bend Resort Park.

Trout fishing is available year-round on the lower Mountain Fork River and just fifteen minutes from our store. Three Rivers Fly Shop offers renowned guided fly fishing services and private schools throughout the year and are committed to provide you with a memorable experience in some of the most beautiful and pristine surroundings imaginable.

*2 Broken Bow Scuba
580 584-3408
lightnin@pine-net.com

Experience scuba diving in the clearest lake in Oklahoma, Broken Bow Lake. Broken Bow Scuba is your full line scuba dealer in this area. We stock Sherwood, Genesis, Akona, Bare, Force Fins, Dive Rite, Deep Sea and lots more. We have rental equipment for certified divers. We do nitrox up to 40% and offer tri-mix and argon for those certified for it. We fill, inspect and hydro tanks, do equipment inspections and repairs and offer scuba lessons. We do guided dives for any skill level either from shore or off of our 30 foot pontoon boat and for those not certified but would like to try the scuba diving experience, we offer a Discover Scuba course. We are located 3.25 miles west of Broken Bow on Hwy 3 then a quarter mile north on Scuba Divers Road. Be sure to check us out while you are in the area.

3 Golf Cedar Creek Golf Course

4 Boating Beavers Bend Marina

5 Hochatown Amusements Located across from the main entrance to the Park (580) 494-6706 or (580) 584-0245
18-hole miniature golf and go-cart track

6 Stephens Gap Raceway

7 Rocket Roller Rink, Idabel (580) 286-3603

8 McCurtain Cinema, Idabel (580) 286-2220

9 A to Z Guest Ranch, Trail Riding
North of Smithville
(580) 244-3729

Things To Do Outside The Park

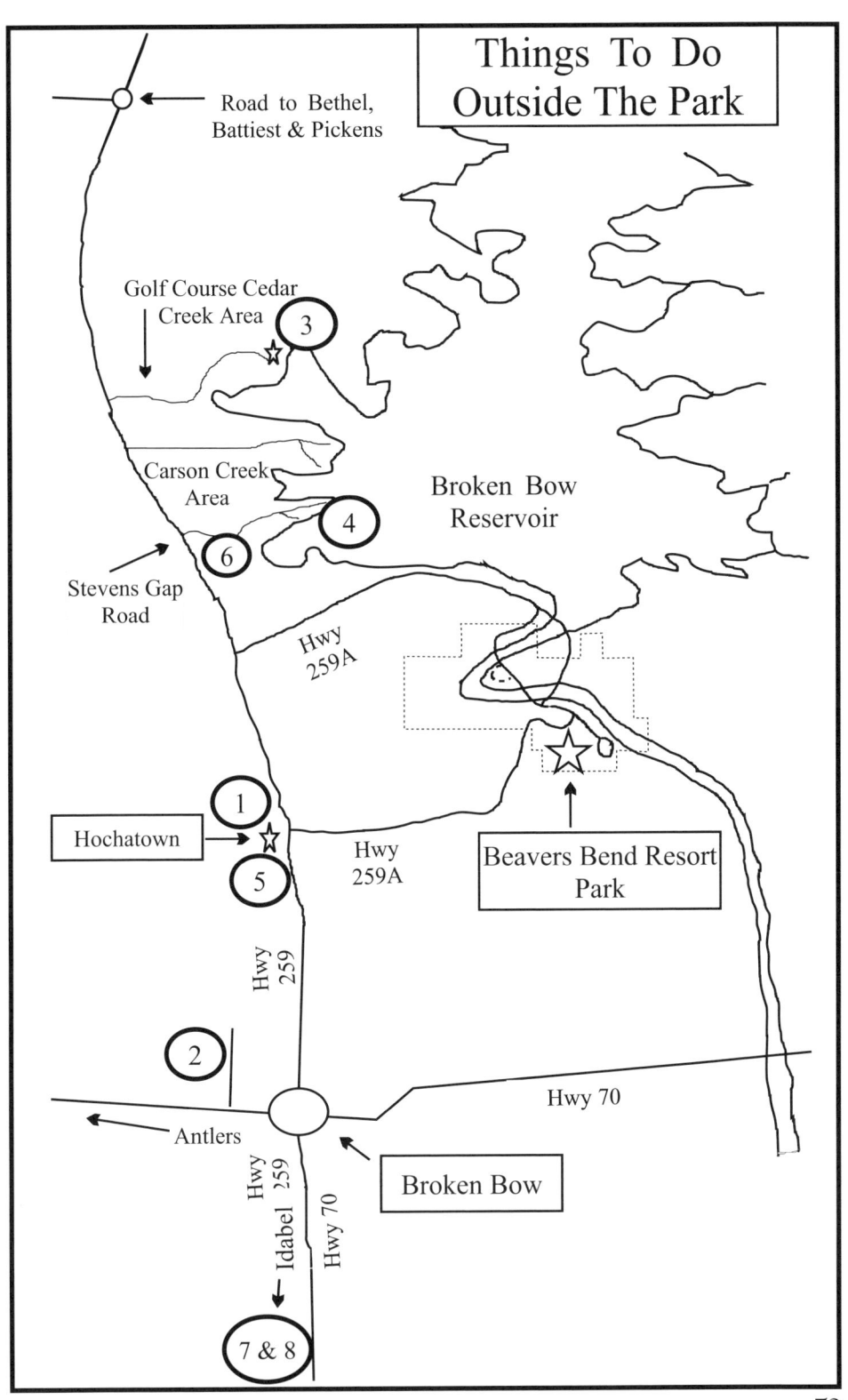

- Road to Bethel, Battiest & Pickens
- Golf Course Cedar Creek Area ③
- Carson Creek Area ④
- ⑥
- Stevens Gap Road
- Broken Bow Reservoir
- Hwy 259A
- Beavers Bend Resort Park
- Hochatown ①
- ⑤
- Hwy 259A
- Hwy 259
- ②
- Antlers
- Hwy 70
- Broken Bow
- Hwy 259 Idabel
- Hwy 70
- ⑦ & ⑧

73

Gift Shops

1 Beavers Bend Resort Park Gift Shop
(580) 494-6509
The gift shop is located within the Park in the same building as the Forest Heritage Center and Park Reservation Center. It has a wide selection of memorable items for you to take home to friends and family. They also have tee shirts, hats, bandanas, bath towels and other items you might find interesting.

2 Crooked River Cabins Gift Shop
(580) 241-5709
After visiting the park and the surrounding area, and if you're ready for a scenic drive, this is a great place for you to visit. Crooked River Cabins Gift Shop is located near the Glover River (their cabins overlook the river). If you have a cell phone call from the Hochatown area for exact directions before you go.

3 Frontier General
Gift shop/gas station/convenience store and restaurant—this is truly one stop shopping. They also carry fishing supplies.

4 Hochatown Junction Gift Shop
(580) 494-6321
If you miss shopping at the mall, then you need to visit Hochatown Junction Gift Shop. Its three gift shops are like shopping at a mini-mall. Here you'll find a unique gift shop, internet coffee house, and a decorative shop with one-of-a-kind prints, etchings, paintings and mirrors all framed and ready to hang.

5 Shady Oak Restaurant/Gift Shop
(580) 494-6210
The gift shop which is part of the restaurant has a wide assortment of unique items including country quilts, pictures, honey, herbs, and vitamins. Where else can you eat breakfast or lunch and shop at the same time?

6 Whip-Poor-Will Resort Gift Shop
(580) 494-6476
We sell the finest fudge for miles around - freshly made with real cream and butter - a small sampling of the varieties of fudge we offer include: chocolate (of course), chocolate pecan, vanilla, amaretto chocolate swirl, mint chocolate swirl, rocky road, butter pecan, maple, peanut butter, cookies and cream, praline, Snickers, Heath, Butterfinger and Almond Joy, and seasonal favorites, just to name a few.
We also have "Made In Oklahoma" Products in our gift shop - candles, soaps, gourmet foods, gift baskets, and other Oklahoma souvenirs.

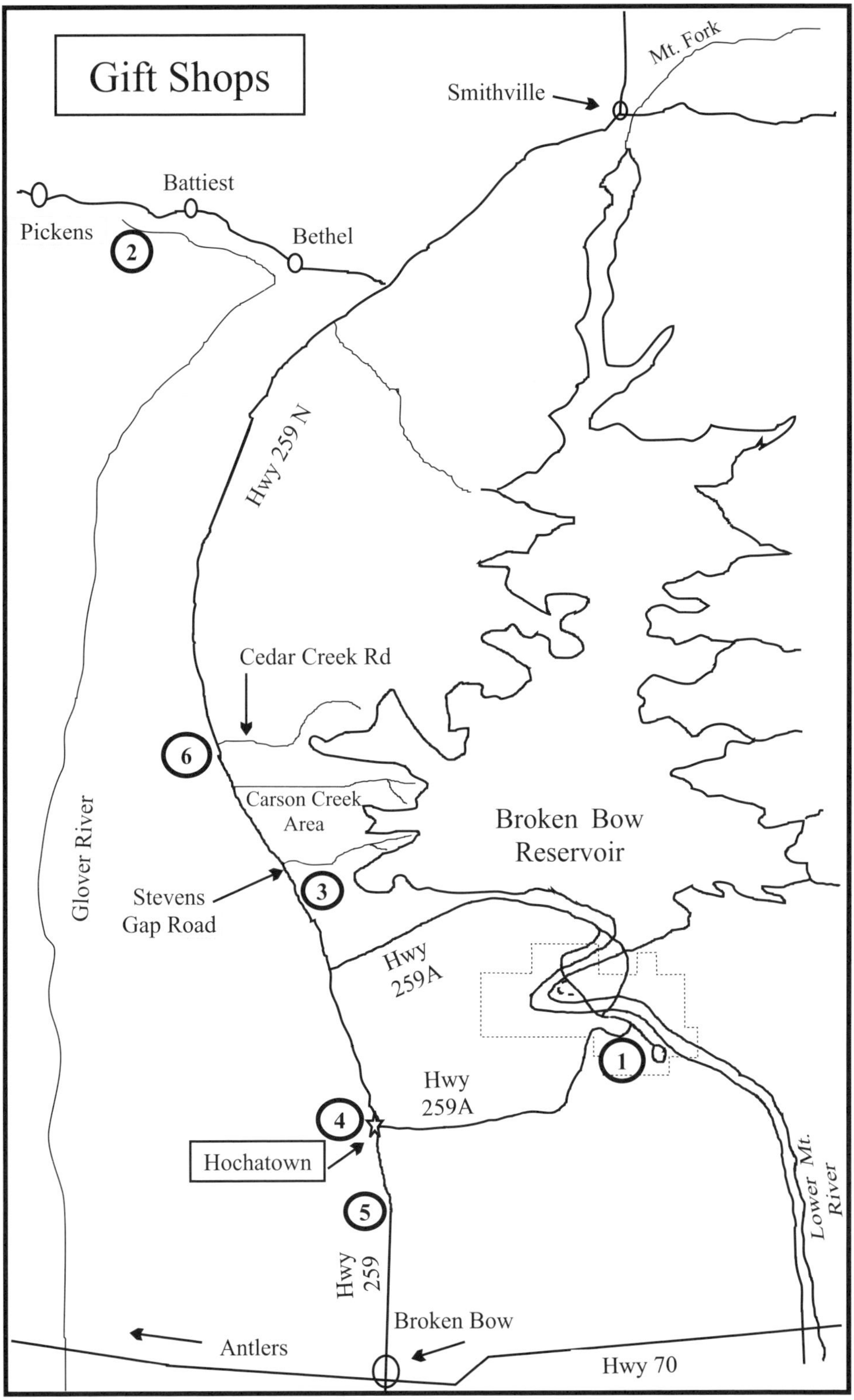
Gift Shops
Smithville
Mt. Fork
Battiest
Pickens
Bethel
2
Hwy 259 N
Cedar Creek Rd
6
Carson Creek
Area
Broken Bow
Reservoir
Glover River
Stevens
Gap Road
3
Hwy
259A
1
Hwy
259A
4
Hochatown
5
Hwy
259
Lower Mt.
River
Broken Bow
Antlers
Hwy 70

Places To Eat

When you get tired of eating pork and beans and cleaning dishes, try dining out at one of the many restaurants in the area surrounding the Park. Mexican, American, Chicken, Pizza, and Oriental are just some of the choices available within ten miles of the park. Following is a listing of restaurants and a map to help you locate them.

Restaurant Guide

1 Abendigo's Grill and Patio
Family Style, Steaks, American
(580) 494-7222
Located in Hochatown on the corner of the Stevens Gap Entrance to the Park. Fine dining at an affordable price, Abendigo has spared no expense to provide a new, modern dining facility to the Beavers Bend area. If you expect the best and are looking for a dining experience you would find in a large city such as Dallas or Tulsa you will feel right at home here. Prices range from very affordable, especially for kids, to what you would expect to pay at a high end restaurant. Menu includes a wide range of offerings from Burgers, Salads, Chicken Fried Steak, to Steak and Shrimp, Filet Mignon, and Lobster.

2 Beavers Bend Restaurant

3 Pier 49 Catfish Restaurant

4 Shady Oak Restaurant / Gift Shop
(580) 494-6210
Family style restaurant with a warm friendly atmosphere that's known for its home-made desserts. If you order breakfast here you won't go away hungry. Shady Oaks chicken strips, chicken fry steak and onion rings are all hand-breaded. The gift shop which is part of the restaurant has a wide assortment of unique items including country quilts, pictures honey, herbs, and vitamins. Open Sun – Thursday 7 am – 3 pm, Friday 7 am – 9 pm and closed Monday.

5 Stephens Gap Restaurant
(580) 494-6350
Located in Hochatown across from the Stevens Gap Entrance to the Park. Affordable down-home cooking and down-home atmosphere you'll feel comfortable no matter what you're wearing. Stevens Gap Restaurant specializes in fresh home made pies and cakes. Their onion rings, shrimp, chicken fry steak and chicken strips are all hand breaded. The catfish, one of the big sellers, is cut in long strips. Open 7 am to 9 pm everyday. You can enjoy your meal in a non-alcohol and smoke free environment.

6 The Oaks Steak House

Places To Eat

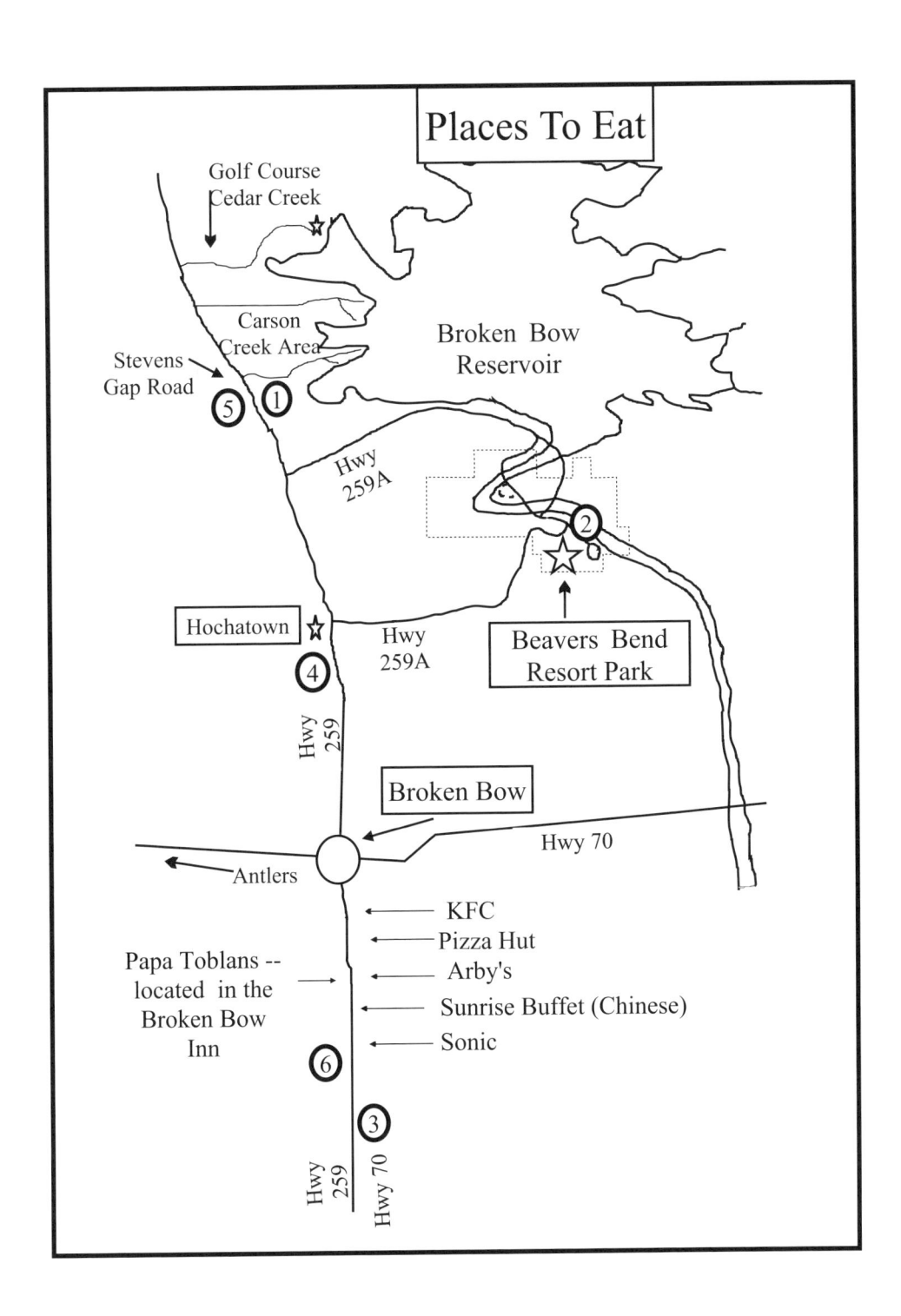

- Golf Course Cedar Creek
- Carson Creek Area
- Stevens Gap Road
- Broken Bow Reservoir
- Hwy 259A
- Hochatown
- Hwy 259A
- Beavers Bend Resort Park
- Hwy 259
- Broken Bow
- Antlers
- Hwy 70
- KFC
- Pizza Hut
- Arby's
- Sunrise Buffet (Chinese)
- Sonic
- Papa Toblans -- located in the Broken Bow Inn
- Hwy 259
- Hwy 70

Other Services You Might Need

Locksmiths

A-1 John's Locksmith 1 (580) 584-1000
1 (580) 584- 6331
1 (580) 584-2980

Rock's Locks 1 (580) 212 5397

Pharmacy
Chandler-Hewitt Drug 1 (580) 584-3378
121 N. Main, Broken Bow 1 (580) 584-6160

Sherrill's Pharmacy 1 (580) 584-3353
101 N. Main, Broken Bow

RV Repair
Robbins RV and ATV Center, Idabel 1 (580) 286-6551
Open: Mon – Fri., 8 AM to 5:50 PM
    Sat., 9 AM to 1 PM

Barbershop
1) Bushwhacker's Hair Salon 1 (580) 584-6888
1/2 Mile S. 259 Broken Bow

Laundromat
2) Suds N' Such Laundry 1 (580) 584-3146
211 N Park Dr.
1 Mile S. 259 Broken Bow

Veterinarians
3) Broken Bow Animal Hospital 1 (580) 584 9101
Boarding Kennel
1Mi. S. Hwy 259 Broken Bow

Stores
4) Wal Mart
5) Pruitt's Grocery Store
GCP gas station/convenience store -
hunting/fishing and land use permits

Propane
6) Cyclo LP Gas Co. Inc. 1 (580) 584-9149

Other Services You Might Need

- Golf Course Cedar Creek
- Carson Creek Area
- Stevens Gap Road
- Broken Bow Reservoir
- Hwy 259A
- Hochatown
- Beavers Bend Resort Park
- Hwy 259
- Broken Bow
- Hwy 70
- Antlers
- ⑤ Pruitt Grocery Store
- ④ Walmart
- ① Bushwhacker's Hair Salon
- ② Suds N' Such Laundry
- ③ Broken Bow Animal Hospital
- Cyclo LP Gas ⑥
- Hwy 259
- Hwy 70
- gcp — Gas Station, Convience Store & Land Use/Fishing Permits

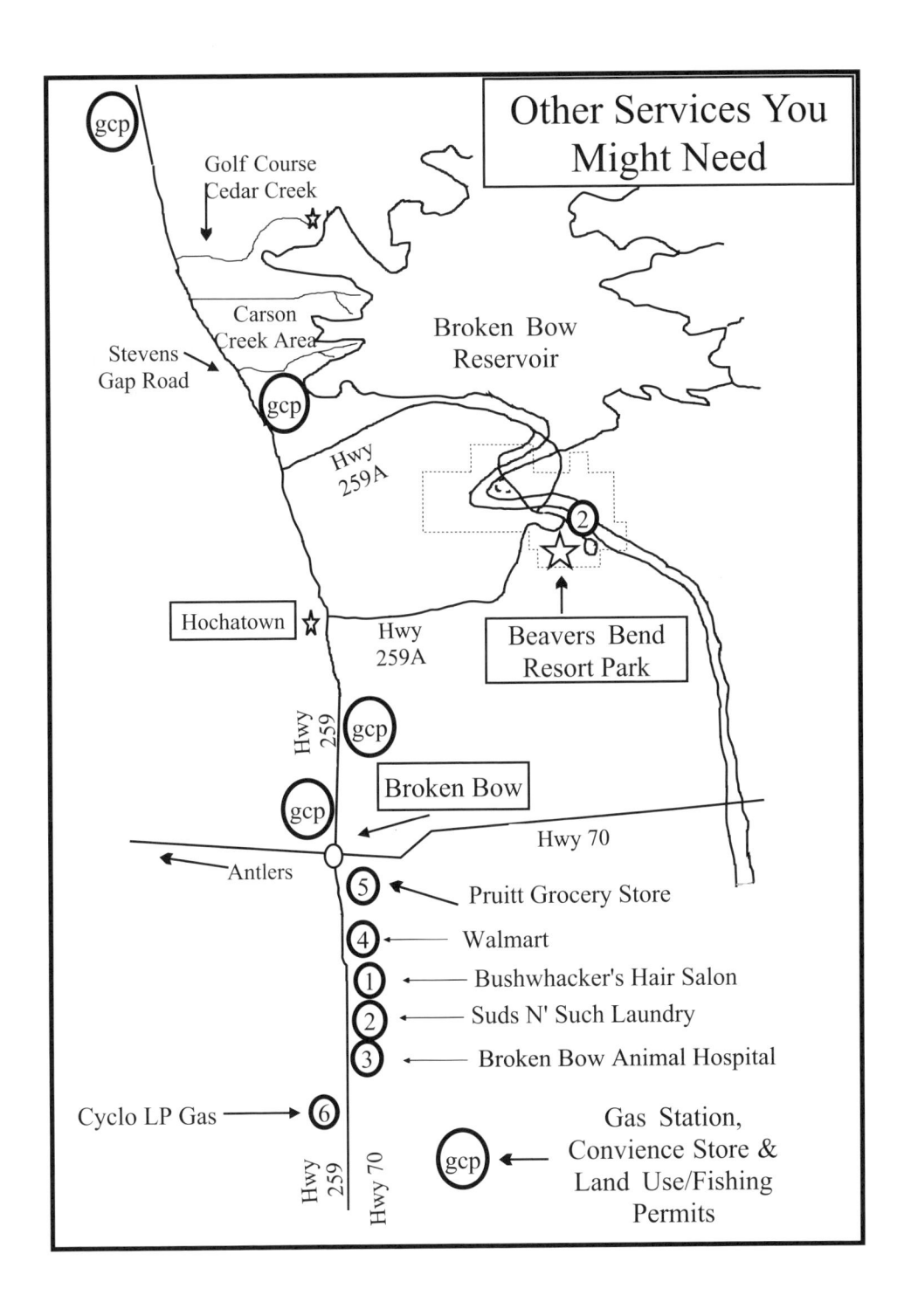

Where to Buy Fishing/Hunting Licenses And Land Access Permits

Fishing/hunting licenses and land access permits can be purchased at most area (X) convenience stores/gas stations and the two area (F) fly-fishing stores.

Church Services

Over the past several years, non-denominational services have been held each Sunday morning at the Forest Heritage Center. Check with the Forest Heritage Reservation Center for exact times of the services.

81

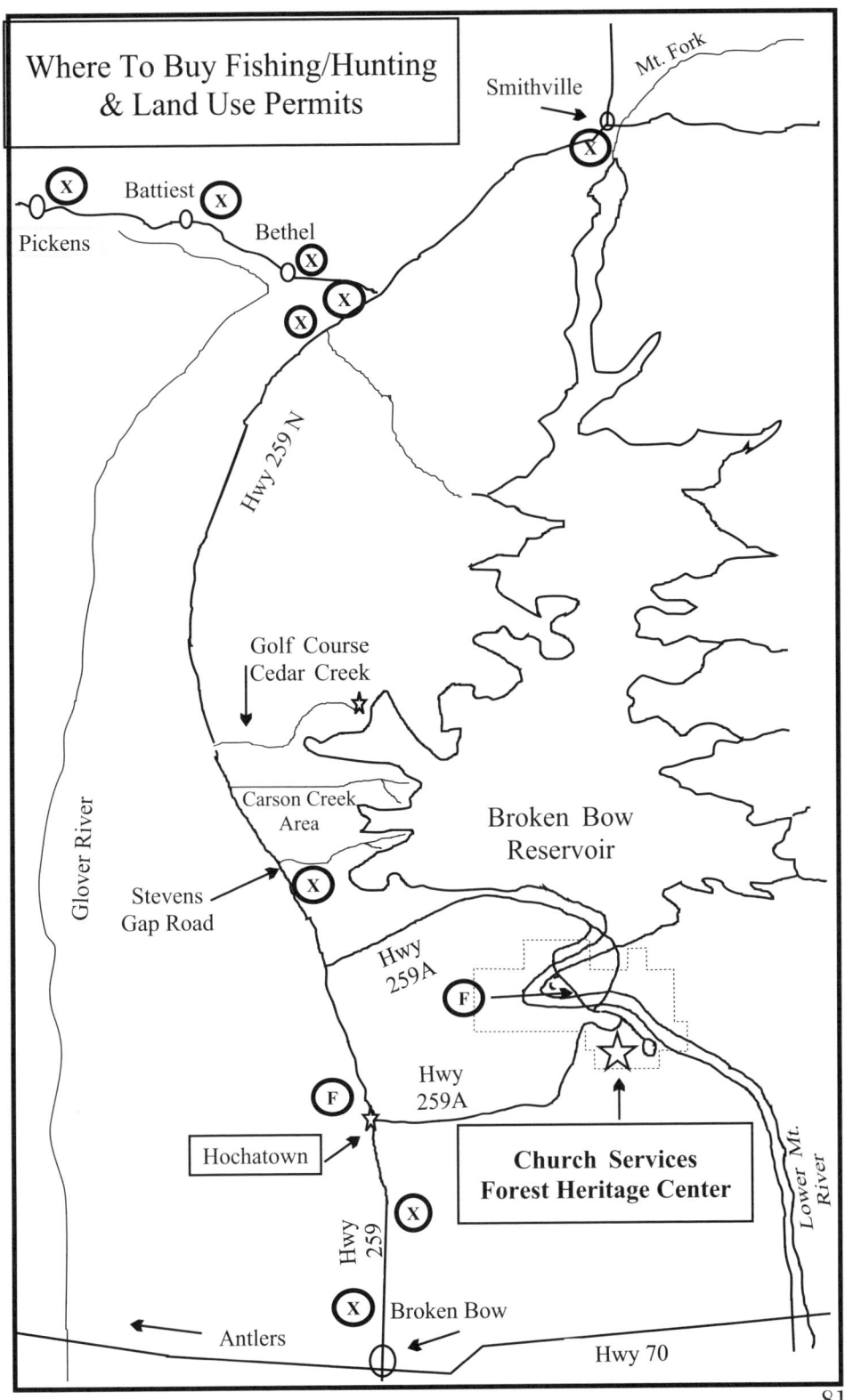

Museums

Beavers Bend Wildlife Museum

Museum of the Red River
Located on the south edge of Idabel.
(580) 286-3616

The Museum of the Red River houses one of the finest and most comprehensive collections of Native American art. The nearly 20,000 objects support a program of changing, interpretative exhibits featuring artifacts found throughout the Americas – North, Central and South- from prehistoric to contemporary times. Especially noteworthy are its regional archaeological materials, ceramics from the American Southwest, featherwork and other crafts from tribal groups living in the Amazon rainforest of South America. Complementary materials from other parts of the world, including Asia, the Pacific Islands, and Africa provide contrasts and comparisons. The museum is also home to a 40 foot long, twelve foot cast of Acrocanthosaurus atokensis, the largest meat eating dinosaur known from the mid-Cretaceous period in North America (125 – 100 million years ago), predating the similarly-sized Tyrannosaurus rex by about forty million years. The original fossil remains were uncovered less than fifteen miles from the museum. The museum sponsors exhibits, lectures, and other programs, and supports ongoing research efforts in the study of American native peoples.

Gardner Mansion and Museum
Seven miles east of Broken Bow on Hwy 70.
(580) 584-6588

The Gardner Mansion and Museum is well-known for their collection of pre-historic and historic Indian and pioneer artifacts. The museum was originally a mansion built in 1884 for Jefferson Gardner who later went on to be the chief of the Choctaw Indians for several years. Also located outside the museum are the remains of a 2,000 year-old Cypress tree.

Gene Autry Museum
Located 4 miles east of Idabel on State Hwy 3.
(580)-286-3747

Located just east of Idabel, this museum has the largest private collection of Gene Autry and Roy Rogers memorabilia in the nation. For a private tour call Albert Frazier. After driving east of Idabel 4 miles on Hwy. 3, turn left just before a trailer park and look for the fourth house on the right.

Animals Native to Southeastern Oklahoma

State Flower: Mistletoe

State Bird: Scissor-Tailed Flycatcher

State Tree: Redbud

The following animals are native to Southeastern Oklahoma and the ones you are most likely to see as you hike the David Boren Hiking Trail or the different Beavers Bend Resort Park Nature Trails. Many people come to this area of Oklahoma to see nature and the animals that make their home in it only to be disappointed. They hike the trails looking for wildlife, but they didn't see any. Remember, that's how the animals stay alive, hiding, staying concealed or scurrying off at the first whiff of scent, sound or movement. Animals are bred through natural selection to survive by blending in or running away long before you can "sneak" up on them. This is their habitat, not ours. So, if you really want to have a chance at seeing some Southeastern Oklahoma wildlife you must first be observant of your surroundings. Second, don't be in a hurry; when hiking a trail remember, you're not in a race to see how quickly you can get to the trails end. Take your time, sit down, look around, remain quiet and try to blend in to your surroundings. Third, but most importantly, just enjoy the experience! Who knows, the animals might come to you.

I remember an experience once when I went deer hunting. I got up early before first light, hiked deep into the woods far from any sign of human life and laid down behind a log that allowed me a great view of a wide open pasture. This was a great place to spot a deer feeding in the early morning. I laid there for over two hours and saw no signs of any animal life. I was obviously very disappointed. Just as I started to get up and return to the camp, I heard a rustling sound in a pile of leaves just on the other side of the log I was hiding behind. Not more than two feet from me was one of the fattest skunks I'd ever seen. Apparently, and thankfully it was unaware of my presence. Sitting there quietly and motionless I watched it waddle off across the field. So, remember, even though you might not see any signs of wildlife be assured, it's really all around you, and sometimes closer than you would like!

Beaver

Beavers found throughout the state weigh from 30 – 60 pounds. Their most identifiable feature is the 9 -10 inch paddle-shaped tail that they slap on the water making a sound similar to a gun shot. The habitat they most prefer is close to streams, lakes and mountain meadows. The beaver's diet consists of bark, cambium, roots and twigs of willows, cottonwoods and other trees. They must continually use their teeth to chew and gnaw on the local trees to prevent their front teeth from growing too long. They construct dams of branches, mud, and vegetation. Their homes, called lodges, are made of the same material and usually have one or more underwater entrances. Their young are called "kits" and remain part of the family until mature, usually 2-4 years.

Eastern Cottontail Rabbit

The Eastern Cottontail can be found throughout the state. They weigh 2 – 4 pounds. Their most identifiable feature is their long 2 -3 inch ears. Their color is generally a grizzled tan, brown and gray mixture with white or light tan on the feet and underside. This rabbit's preferred habitat is edge cover, brush, creek bottoms, briar patches and swamps. Their diet consists of leafy vegetation in summer and bark and twigs of woody vegetation in winter. They stay busy having between 3 to 5 litters a year each consisting of from 4 to 7 young. The young leave their nest within 3 weeks of being born.

Porcupine

Found mostly in the forested eastern part of the state, porcupines are between 25-31 inches long including a 7-9 inch tail, weigh 10-30 pounds and are coated overall with their very identifiable overlay of yellow-tipped hairs and thickly set sharp spines that dislodge easily. Despite many people's beliefs they do not throw their spines at attackers, in defense they curl up in a ball offering the attacker only a mouth full of their long sharp spines. The porcupine's diet consists of inner bark, small twigs, bark of Pines, Poplar, and other trees. They have a keen sense of smell and hearing. Their dens can be found in hollow trees or almost any place where it can get out of the weather. Their new-born young, usually 1 to 2, are well-developed at birth and are able to climb trees and eat solid food a few hours after birth.

Opossum

Opossums are found throughout the state preferring to stay in woodland areas. They weigh between 4-12 pounds, look like oversized rats and are the only pouched mammal to be found in North America. Their diet consists of fruits, insects and small mammals. The Opossum's den can be found in hollow trees, under buildings, etc. They have large litters consisting of 8-18 young that stay attached in the belly pouch for up to 70 days. When crowded out of the pouch the young will cling to the coarse coat of their mother until reaching 2 months of age before leaving. When confronted with danger the Opossum often feigns death.

Armadillo

Armadillo's can be found statewide. They weigh 8-17 pounds and are covered in a dark gray or sooty black flexible armor plate. Their diet consists of insects but they will eat fruits. They give birth to one litter of 4 each spring.

Skunk

In Oklahoma you might see either Striped or Spotted Skunks. The Striped Skunk weighs about 6 – 10 pounds while its smaller cousin only weighs 1 – 1 ½ pounds. Skunks are found almost everywhere; woods, plains, swamps, meadows, suburbs and countryside. Diet consists of rats, mice, chipmunks, insects, fruits, berries and bird eggs. They dens are under buildings and in burrows. They bare 4 and 10 young at birth in the spring and the family will break up in the fall.

Raccoon

Raccoons found statewide, weigh 8-35 pounds. Their body, covered with a dense fur, ranges from yellow in color to almost black. They have an identifiable darker mask on the face. Their diet includes fish, crayfish, frogs, fruit, vegetables, insects, eggs and poultry. The raccoon's den can be found in hollow trees or dry caverns among rocks. They are nocturnal, meaning they usually only come out at night. Their litters consist of between 2 to 6 young born only 60 days after mating. The young leave the nest after 2 months and the family breaks up after the young are 1 year old.

Coyote

Found statewide the coyote reaches a shoulder height of about 21 inches and weighs between 20-50 pounds. Its preferred habitat is open plains with occasional brush thickets and former forest land that has been opened up. Their diet consists of fruits and vegetables, rodents, birds, and insects. Rabbit is the coyote's favorite food. They den in caves, rock shelters, hollow trees or burrows dug in the ground. Young are born blind, helpless and covered with short, dark fur. The young leave the den area at 3 months and by fall are on their own ranging as much as 100 miles from their birthplace.

Bobcat

Bobcats can be found throughout the state. They weigh between 15-20 pounds and are a pale brown to reddish brown with black streaks and spots above. Their preferred habitat is bottomland forests, canyons and mountains. Bobcats are most active at night. Their diet includes rats, mice, rabbits, snakes, birds, and occasionally small domestic livestock and poultry. They mate once a year, in late winter and after 2 months give birth to 2 kittens. The young are weaned at 2 months and the family breaks up in 6-7 months.

Red Bat

The small red bat is 4 inches in length and weighs only ¼ to ½ ounce. It ranges through the state. It is brick-red or rusty-red in color. The Bat roosts in trees and caves. It will leave its roost at dusk to feed on insects captured in flight. The Red Bat emits sounds and listens for the echo to detect its prey. They usually have 3-4 young that cling to their mother and nurse until they become too heavy for her to fly

Whitetail Deer

The whitetail deer stands 3-3½ feet tall at shoulder height and weighs between 120-160 pounds. Their color varies and changes with the seasons. The bucks grow antlers which are shed yearly. The whitetail deer's preferred habitat is woodlands, forest edges, and second growth forests. Diet is grass, bark, twigs, acorns, domestic crops and young shoots of trees and other plants. They get their name from showing their large tails white underside while running. The females give birth in the late spring to 1 or 2 fawns.

Wild Turkey

The turkey, located in the eastern part of the state, weighs 15-27 pounds. They have extremely good hearing and eyesight and for this reason are very challenging to hunt. Their diet consists of acorns, berries, insects, and domestic crops such as peanuts, and corn. The hen lays 8-15 cream colored eggs spotted with reddish brown and lilac from late March to early June.

Black Bear

Measuring 4-6 feet in length, 2-3 feet height at shoulder and weighing between 150-400 pounds the black bear is the largest animal to be found in Southeastern Oklahoma. Black bears are normally very shy and are not active predators. They live mainly in inaccessible forests, swamps, and brushy areas. Their diet consists of nuts, berries, grasses, insects, eggs, honey, and small animals. Bears hibernate in winter in caves, hollow logs, large trees, or beneath boulders. They give birth to 1 or 2 cubs in the winter. The cubs leave at the end of the second winter.

Eastern Fox and Eastern Gray Squirrel

Two types of squirrels are found in Southeastern Oklahoma. The Eastern Fox Squirrel is the larger of the two weighing from 1-3 pounds. The Eastern Gray, much smaller, weighs less then 1½ pounds. Both can be found in hardwood forests and city parks. They diet on acorns, hickory nuts and seeds. Normally 3-5 young are born in leafy nests or a tree hollow. The young leave the nest at six weeks.

Bobwhite Quail

Average length of the Bobwhite Quail is 10 inches and they weigh about 6 ounces. They can be found statewide in edge cover areas where open fields meet woods or thickets. Their diet consists of insects, various weed seeds and some domestic grains. They lay 14-16 white eggs in well-hollowed nests of dry grasses, straw, weed stalks and bark strips. Nests are usually located along overgrown fence rows or in neglected corners of fields. Quail remain in groups called "coveys" except during breeding season.

About Outback Guides

Outback Guides has been in business over thirty years guiding groups to many of the most wilderness areas in the United States. Yellowstone, Rocky Mountain National Park, the Grand Canyon and Wrangell National Park in Alaska are just a small sample of wilderness areas Outback Guides has traveled to. Recently we have added trips to Peru, White Water Rafting in Colorado and Canoe trips in the isolated Quetico National Park located in Canada.

Outback Guides also sells and rents Backpacking, Camping, Hiking, and Mountain Climbing equipment. Visit our web site at www.outbackguides.com for detailed information on trips and outdoor equipment. To order copies of this book call 1(918) 446-5956 or email us at outback@outbackguides.com

About Billy Dennis

Outback Guides, owned by Billy Dennis, has been in business since 1965. Billy is the current President of Fiends of Beavers Bend Resort Park, a non-profit organization that is involved in promoting the nature aspects of the park and working with the State Department of Tourism and Recreation to build a new nature center in the park. He has also taken on the responsibility of park trail maintenance and construction since 1978.

Billy has been guiding wilderness trips for over thirty five years. He has worked with many different diverse groups: youth, professional, private clients, senior citizens and Boy Scout and Girl Scout troops. Billy also conducts seminars on a variety of wilderness subjects to area schools, clubs, and even the Oklahoma state forest rangers. Gray wolves of Yellowstone, bears of North America, environmental culture, Triangle Camping, LNT, and basics of hiking and camping are just some of the seminars that Billy conducts.
Billy has backpacking experience in just about every national park in the country and many state parks.

About Dave White

Dave White is an experienced educator and trainer in the fields of teaching and learning, and education reform. He has taught a variety of subjects and has recently retired after spending the last 25 years teaching within the OSU System. He currently teaches as an adjunct at Tulsa Community College, and organizes and guides high adventure trips to places such as Peru, Yellowstone, the Grand Canyon, and canoe trips in isolated wilderness areas of Canada. Dave has also been a Boy Scout troop leader and for years worked with young people taking them on camping trips. He has undergraduate and graduate degrees from the State University of New York – Geneseo, and graduate hours in Guidance and Counseling from Northeastern State University in Oklahoma.